To
Lorna
and Fred and Viv,
fellow island travellers

Contents

Work

Transport

Introduction

There are 790 Scottish islands, according to VisitScotland, which used to be called the Scottish Tourist Board. So that's it. No argument. But it really depends on how you define an island and there is more than one definition. Does the land become an island only if it is totally surrounded by water and the only way to get to or from it is by boat or plane – or, if you are bold or daft enough, by swimming? In that case, islands that are connected to each other or to the mainland by a bridge or a causeway would be ruled out. It would be goodbye to Skye as an island. Because they are linked, North and South Uist and Benbecula could no longer be thought of as three separate islands. And the likes of Vatersay, Scalpay, Seil, South Ronaldsay and others wouldn't count as separate islands. So defining an island in such terms would be a foolish approach.

The General Register Office for Scotland, in its 2001 census of Scotland's inhabited islands, published on 23 November 2003, says that islands are still classified as individual islands even when they are linked to another island or to the mainland by connections such as a bridge, causeway or ford. Its official definition of an island is this: 'An island is a mass of land surrounded by water, separate from the Scottish mainland.'

Hamish Haswell-Smith, in his excellent *The Scottish Islands: A Comprehensive Guide to Every Scottish Island*, says there are 165 Scottish islands. He had to cut down the total, not surprisingly, because he planned to visit every one of them for his book. So he settled for those above a certain size and that was forty hectares and over – i.e. about one hundred acres or one-sixth of a square mile or more. He said he had very restrictive rules of classification and defined an island thus: 'An island is a piece of land or group of pieces of land which is entirely surrounded by seawater at lowest astronomical tide and to which there is no permanent means of dry access.' He mentions the tide because the size of an island will change with every ebb and flow of the tide. He added a final requirement for his definition – the water surrounding the island had to be sea water. That takes out a large swathe of islands – Loch Lomond, for example, has no fewer than twenty-three islands which deserve to be included in any book about the Scottish islands. For Hamish to visit all 165 of his chosen islands was a splendid achievement and his book is an encyclopaedia for island-philes. I certainly do not claim to have completed an odyssey that matches his but, in my research for the offbeat and interesting facts about Scottish islands, not one of the 790 has been ruled out.

Having established that there are 790 Scottish islands, it might be expected that I should now do you the courtesy of telling you where they all are. But this is not a gazetteer or a tourist manual and you have to be something of an anorak to be genuinely interested in the exact location of each of the 790. However, I will do my best to give you an outline of where most of them are and what they are called and you are invited to delve much deeper into this book for a distillation and classification of the weird and wonderful, fascinating and downright interesting facts and fiction about the Scottish islands. Don't forget that they all belong to us – they are part of our heritage, part of our greater island story.

Let's start at the top – geographically speaking. **Shetland** has about 100 islands and **Orkney** has sixty-seven. Shetland and Orkney were under Norse rule for centuries. In 1468, the Orkney Islands became part of Scotland when they were included in the dowry on James III of Scotland's marriage to Princess Margaret of Denmark–Norway. A year later, Margaret's father, Christian I, could not pay the balance of the dowry and he pledged his land and rights in Shetland to make up the shortfall.

The Outer and Inner Hebrides cover 2,812 square miles and have more than 500 islands between them. The name Hebrides comes from the Norse *havbredey*, meaning 'isles on the edge of the sea'.

The Outer Hebrides, better known as the Western Isles and also known as the Long Isle – although there are, in fact, more than 200 of them – are the heartland of Gaelic culture. They extend to 130 miles, from the Butt of Lewis in the north to Barra Head in the south. Lewis is the largest and the rest of them are Harris, North Uist, Benbecula, South Uist, Barra, Berneray, Baleshare, Grimsay, Scalpay, St Kilda (really a name for a group of islands), Eriskay and Vatersay. Five miles west of North Uist and Benbecula are five small islands and several drying rocks which form the Monach Islands group, also known by the Norse name Husker. These islands are connected to each other at low tide. They were inhabited until the 1930s when the last remaining families moved to North Uist.

Included in the Inner Hebrides are two of Scotland's main islands – Skye and Mull – as well as Raasay, Iona, Staffa, Islay, the Treshnish Isles, Lismore, Kerrera, Seil, Easdale, Luing, Jura, Rum, Eigg, Coll, Tiree, Canna, Colonsay and Oronsay (you can walk from Colonsay to Oronsay when the tide is out). Eigg, Muck, Rum and Canna, which lie to the south of Skye, are sometimes listed separately as the Small Islands and there is a string of uninhabited islands west of Luing which are known as the Garvellachs. One of them, Eilach an Naoimh (Holy Isle), is where the Celtic missionary Brendan the Navigator founded a community in 542, twenty-one years before St Columba landed on Iona. Treshnish is an archipelago of uninhabited islands north-west of Staffa, the main one being Lunga.

The islands of the Clyde are Arran, Bute (it just makes it as an island – it is separated from the Cowal peninsula by a slither of water), Great Cumbrae and Little Cumbrae. And, in the east of Scotland, there are the Firth of Forth Islands, a number of separate islands or island groups, principally Inchmickery (together with the nearby Cow and Calves) off Edinburgh, Fidra, Lamb and Craigleith, plus the Bass Rock off North Berwick and the much larger Isle of May in the outer part of the Firth.

It is a sad fact that the bulk of British holidaymakers and travellers – and that, of course, includes the Scots – are more familiar with the Canary Islands than with the islands off the west coast of Scotland. Quiz them about Lanzarote, Fuerteventura, Tenerife and Gomera and they will be full of praise and knowledge and be quick to pull out the holiday snaps. But ask them what they think about Berneray, Eriskay, Vatersay, Coll, Tiree, Hoy or Yell and there will be a glazed look on their faces. It is their loss. Scotland's islands are a veritable treasure trove of beauty, heritage, peace, solitude and surprises and, for many people, the most romantic of Scottish islands is Skye. Its strong tourism industry is based primarily on nostalgic, historic associations, the Gaelic culture and the rugged scenery. But forgive me, Skye, despite what the General Register Office for Scotland says, you ceased to be an island and lost that island magic with the building of the Skye Bridge in 1995.

Mull, one of the larger islands, is encrusted by 300 miles of rugged coastline and retains that magic. Mull was known to the classical Greeks and Ptolemy, the ancient astronomer and geographer who lived in Alexandria in the second century CE, referred to it as Maleus. It is enhanced by the islands within its reach such as Iona, Ulva, Lunga (also known as the Puffin Island), Gometra and Staffa. St Columba founded his church at Iona in 563. The graveyard on Iona was the burial place of all the Scottish kings up to the time of Duncan and Macbeth in the eleventh century. The cemetery is said to hold the graves of forty-eight Scottish, four Irish, eight Norwegian and two French kings. But the gravestones have long since been defaced or destroyed.

Mendelssohn visited Staffa and its spectacular Fingal's Cave in 1829 and was inspired to write his *Hebrides Overture*.

Arran is one of the most southerly of the Scottish islands and it is known as 'Scotland in miniature' because it is seen as a condensed version of the rest of Scotland, with mountains and lochs to the north, rolling hills and meadows in the south and a stunning coastline. It has ten peaks over 2,000 feet. It was inhabited before the dawn of recorded history and it has the ancient stones and burial cairns to prove it. The Irish Scots came over and settled in the early sixth century, making Arran part of the Kingdom of Dalriada. The Vikings held it for a while until they were ousted by Somerled, Lord of the Isles, who was possibly of Norse descent.

South Uist is the largest and most stunning of the southern chain of the Outer Hebrides islands and, like so many of the islands, it has parts of its past it wants to banish from its memory. Its people were subjected to terrible assaults during the Highland Clearances. In only three years – 1849 to 1851 – more than 2,000 islanders were forcibly drafted onto ships bound for Quebec. Those who resisted were hunted down like animals, tied up and flung onto the ships.

Colonsay is one of the most remote of the islands of Argyll. It is a naturalist's paradise and was once an important Viking stronghold. It is joined at low water to the smaller island of Oronsay and they are separated by a wide expanse of shell sand called the Strand. You can walk across when the tide is out or you can hitch a lift on the Post Office bus. Halfway across is what they called the Sanctuary Cross – any Colonsay fugitive who reached it was immune from punishment provided he stayed on Oronsay for a year and a day. St Columba is said to have landed on Colonsay on his way to Iona from Ireland in the middle of the sixth century. The surprise is that he did not decide to stay there but he was no doubt correct in believing that his destiny lay on another Scottish island, despite the charms of Colonsay.

That's what the Scottish islands are all about. They beckon you and, once you get there, they entice you to stay on – but you know that there are so many more you have to visit because they all have something different to offer.

It can take a lifetime.

Some Facts and Figures

Iona Abbey

Scottish Islands Census

According to *Scotland's Census 2001, Statistics for Inhabited Islands*, which was published in November 2002, there were 3,129 fewer people living on the ninety-six inhabited Scottish islands in 2001, compared to 1991. The census also revealed that twice as many islands lost population as gained, fewer islanders got married, more survived to a much older age, more lived alone and 1,000 left for the mainland. The islands census, which includes islands that are joined to the mainland or other islands by a bridge, causeway or ford, presents a fascinating statistical snapshot of Scottish island life.

The total population of the islands is almost 100,000, ranging from nearly 20,000 people living in Lewis and Harris to one person living on each of Innischonan, Sanda, Shuna and Eilean Donan. There are thirty-five islands, including Skye and the mainland of Orkney, whose population increased. A total of 99,739 people live on the islands, representing 2% of the population of Scotland. A total of sixty-four islands experienced a fall in population between 1991 and 2001. Of the fourteen islands with populations of over 1,000 people, only 4% of them (mainland Orkney, Skye, Arran and Great Cumbrae) increased their population. And the most populous of the islands in 2001 was Lewis and Harris, with a population of 19,918, which was around 8% fewer than in 1991.

The island groups which had the highest proportion of people who have reached retirement age were Lismore (39.7%) and Great Cumbrae (36.9%) while Eigg (9.2%) and Trondra (5.3%) had the lowest.

On the islands, 49.2% of the residents in 2001 were male, slightly higher than the figure of 48.1% for Scotland as a whole. There were twenty-eight island groups that had more male residents than female, compared with twenty-two which had more females.

Only two island groups gained more than ten persons.

ISLANDS GALORE

Table 1 Number of residents and households in all inhabited islands

Island group and island	Total residents			Total households		Hectares
	1981	1991	2001	1991	2001	
Scotland	5,035,315	4,998,567	5,062,011	2,020,050	2,192,246	7,813,262
All inhabited islands	100,329	102,868	99,739	40,105	43,327	1,024,648
Argyll & Bute	*15,660*	*16,055*	*15,902*	*6,920*	*7,489*	*233,856*
Combined with mainland	61	70	67	23	29	2,708
Danna	7	1	5	1	2	315
Davaar	4	-	2	-	1	52
Inchmurrin	7	10	13	5	5	133
Inchtavannach	4	4	3	1	1	52
Innischonan	1	16	1	5	1	783
Kerrera	38	39	42	11	18	1,234
Sanda	-	-	1	-	1	139
Bute	*7,311*	*7,354*	*7,228*	*3,378*	*3,570*	*12,429*
Bute	7,306	7,354	7,228	3,378	3,570	12,168
Inchmarnock	5	-	-	-	-	261
Coll	*131*	*172*	*164*	*75*	*80*	*7,723*
Colonsay	*136*	*106*	*113*	*50*	*55*	*4,912*
Colonsay	133	98	108	48	52	4,336
Oronsay	3	8	5	2	3	576
Easdale 1	*32*	*41*	*58*	*20*	*28*	*24*
Gigha	*153*	*143*	*110*	*62*	*51*	*1,368*
Iona	*122*	*130*	*125*	*43*	*57*	*855*
Islay	*3,792*	*3,538*	*3,457*	*1,419*	*1,541*	*61,497*
Jura	*228*	*196*	*188*	*79*	*89*	*36,543*
Lismore	*129*	*140*	*146*	*64*	*72*	*2,244*
Luing 4	*167*	*183*	*220*	*93*	*103*	*2,238*
Luing	157	179	212	91	99	1,440
Lunga (Luing)	3	2	7	-	3	259
Shuna (Luing) 4	7	1	1	1	1	438

Island group and island	Total residents			Total households		Hectares
	1981	1991	2001	1991	2001	
Torsa	-	1	-	1	-	101
Mull	*2,214*	*2,708*	*2,696*	*1,095*	*1,221*	*91,718*
Erraid	-	-	8	-	5	229
Gometra	4	-	5	-	2	490
Mull	2,197	2,678	2,667	1,084	1,208	89,111
Ulva	13	30	16	11	6	1,888
Seil 1	*424*	*506*	*560*	*208*	*254*	*1,405*
Tiree	*760*	*768*	*770*	*311*	*339*	*8,191*
Skerryvore	3	-	-	-	-	1
Tiree	757	768	770	311	339	8,191
Eilean Siar	***30,711***	***29,600***	***26,502***	***10,970***	***11,275***	***306,916***
Barra	*1,264*	*1,244*	*1,078*	*446*	*462*	*6,173*
Benbecula	*1,887*	*1,803*	*1,249*	*571*	*502*	*8,498*
Benbecula	1,869	1,771	1,219	560	491	8,235
Flodda	7	8	11	4	4	145
Grimsay (South)	11	24	19	7	7	117
Berneray (North Uist)	*133*	*141*	*136*	*68*	*68*	*1,056*
Eriskay	*210*	*179*	*133*	*67*	*66*	*754*
Great Bernera	*278*	*262*	*233*	*108*	*110*	*2,240*
Grimsay (North)	*204*	*215*	*201*	*79*	*83*	*1,146*
Lewis and Harris	*22,485*	*21,737*	*19,918*	*8,224*	*8,506*	*217,820*
Lewis and Harris	22,476	21,737	19,918	8,224	8,506	217,186
St Kilda (or Hirta)	9	-	-	-	-	633
North Uist	*1,466*	*1,459*	*1,320*	*550*	*579*	*35,479*
North Uist	1,399	1,404	1,271	530	561	34,464

continued

Island group and island	Total residents			Total households s		Hectares
	1981	1991	2001	1991	2001	
Baleshare	67	55	49	20	18	1,015
Scalpay (Harris)	*455*	*382*	*322*	*146*	*140*	*702*
South Uist	*2,231*	*2,106*	*1,818*	*688*	*723*	*32,094*
Vatersay	*107*	*72*	*94*	*23*	*36*	*953*
Fife	***4***	***2***	***2***	***1***	***1***	***85***
Combined with mainland	*4*	*2*	*2*	*1*	*1*	*85*
Inchcolm	2	2	2	1	1	12
May	2	-	-	-	-	73
Highland	***7,608***	***9,199***	***9,603***	***3,589***	***4,105***	***192,591***
Combined with mainland	*41*	*27*	*27*	*11*	*9*	*1,957*
Carna	-	4	-	1	-	183
Dry (or Eilean Tioram)	9	1	-	1	-	7
Eilean Donan	-	-	1	-	1	5
Ewe	11	12	12	4	4	374
Isle Martin	1	1	-	1	-	136
Shona (or Eilean Shona)	12	9	9	4	3	714
Tanera Mor	8	-	5	-	1	538
Eigg	*119*	*141*	*131*	*56*	*63*	*15,735*
Canna	11	20	6	7	3	1,148
Eigg	64	69	67	29	31	2,967
Hyskier (or Oigh-Sgeir)	-	2	-	-	-	49
Muck	20	24	30	10	15	541
Rhum	17	26	22	10	11	10,826
Sanday (Canna)	7	-	6	-	3	203
Raasay	*155*	*163*	*194*	*78*	*93*	*7,329*
Raasay	152	163	192	78	92	6,282
Rona (Skye)	3	-	2	-	1	1,047

Island group and island	Total residents			Total households		Hectares
	1981	1991	2001	1991	2001	
Skye	*7,293*	*8,868*	*9,251*	*3,444*	*3,940*	*167,570*
Eilean Ban	2	-	2	-	1	10
Ornsay	5	4	-	2	-	38
Pabay	3	-	-	-	-	198
Scalpay (Skye)	6	7	10	2	4	2,499
Skye	7,268	8,843	9,232	3,435	3,932	163,785
Soay	8	14	7	5	3	1,040
North Ayrshire Combined with mainland	**5,151**	**5,873**	**6,492**	**2,560**	**3,002**	**44,512**
Little Cumbrae	6	6	-	4	-	278
Arran	*3,845*	*4,474*	*5,058*	*1,870*	*2,247*	*43,079*
Arran	3,845	4,472	5,045	1,869	2,247	42,801
Holy Island	-	-	13	-	-	264
Pladda	-	2	-	1	-	14
Great Cumbrae	*1,300*	*1,393*	*1,434*	*686*	*755*	*1,155*
Orkney Islands	**18,419**	**19,612**	**19,245**	**7,695**	**8,342**	**99,093**
Burray	*283*	*363*	*357*	*135*	*146*	*1,007*
Eday	*147*	*166*	*121*	*79*	*65*	*2,773*
Flotta	*178*	*126*	*81*	*51*	*39*	*976*
Hoy 3	*461*	*450*	*392*	*199*	*197*	*14,375*
Mainland of Orkney 3	*14,029*	*15,155*	*15,339*	*5,951*	*6,615*	*51,102*
Cava	2	2	-	1	-	112
Gairsay	6	3	3	1	1	257
Graemsay	21	27	21	11	11	393
Mainland of Orkney 2	14,000	15,123	15,315	5,938	6,603	50,340

continued

Island group and island	Total residents			Total households		Hectares
	1981	1991	2001	1991	2001	
North Ronaldsay	*109*	*92*	*70*	*36*	*36*	*780*
Papa Westray	*92*	*85*	*65*	*35*	*30*	*840*
Rousay	*253*	*291*	*267*	*113*	*115*	*5,664*
Egilsay	23	46	37	13	11	581
Rousay	209	217	212	92	97	4,805
Wyre	21	28	18	8	7	278
Sanday (Orkney)	*525*	*533*	*478*	*204*	*206*	*5,306*
Shapinsay	*329*	*322*	*300*	*129*	*127*	*2,817*
South Ronaldsay	*891*	*943*	*854*	*353*	*363*	*4,973*
Stronsay	*420*	*382*	*358*	*143*	*148*	*3,670*
Auskerry	-	-	5	-	1	55
Papa Stronsay	-	-	10	-	1	83
Stronsay	420	382	343	143	146	3,532
Westray	*702*	*704*	*563*	*267*	*255*	*4,811*
Sule Skerry	1	-	-	-	-	19
Westray	701	704	563	267	255	4,792
Perth & Kinross	***3***	***3***	***3***	***1***	***1***	***46***
Combined with mainland						
Moncrieffe (or Friarton)	3	3	3	1	1	46
Shetland Islands	***22,768***	***22,522***	***21,988***	***8,368***	***9,111***	***147,357***
Bressay	*334*	*352*	*384*	*138*	*161*	*3,106*
East Burra	*78*	*72*	*66*	*25*	*28*	*540*
Fair Isle	*58*	*67*	*69*	*22*	*26*	*815*

Island group and island	Total residents			Total households		Hectares
	1981	1991	2001	1991	2001	
Fetlar	101	90	86	39	42	4,144
Housay	82	85	76	29	32	203
Bruray	33	27	26	9	11	52
Housay	49	58	50	20	21	152
Mainland of Shetland	17,755	17,596	17,575	6,627	7,314	98,175
Mainland of Shetland	17,722	17,562	17,550	6,615	7,305	96,997
Papa Stour	33	33	23	11	8	883
Vaila	-	1	2	1	1	295
Muckle Roe	99	115	104	39	39	1,730
Trondra	93	117	133	35	46	271
Unst	1,140	1,055	720	371	321	12,557
West Burra	806	857	784	290	309	2,076
Foula	39	40	31	14	17	1,286
West Burra	767	817	753	276	292	790
Whalsay	1,031	1,041	1,034	336	376	2,111
Yell	1,191	1,075	957	417	417	21,629
South Ayrshire	**2**	**-**	**-**	**-**	**-**	**89**
Combined with mainland						
Ailsa Craig	2	-	-	-	-	89
Stirling	**3**	**2**	**2**	**1**	**1**	**103**
Combined with mainland						
Inchfad	3	2	2	1	1	103

* **Source:** *Scotland's Census 2001, Statistics for Inhabited Islands.* Data supplied by the General Register Office for Scotland. Crown Copyright.

Those of which lost the most ground were Lewis and Harris and mainland Shetland, both of which had a net migration loss of more than 100 people. Since they were both populous islands, however, this represented less than 1% of their respective populations.

While one in fifty Scots are from a non-white ethnic background, only one in 150 islanders are. The non-white ethnic population was higher in 2001 in both Scotland and the islands than it was in 1991. On the islands, numbers increased by almost 60% from 405 people in 1991 to 645 people in 2001.

As to country of birth, in Scotland as a whole 87% of persons in 2001 were born in Scotland. For the islands, this figure was lower at 84%.

The proportion of islanders who were born in England (13%) was substantially higher than the proportion of persons in Scotland who were born there (8%). A total of fifteen island groups had at least a quarter of their population born in England – and thirteen of these fifteen island groups were in Argyll and Bute or the Orkney Islands.

Not surprisingly, the proportion of people aged three or over who speak Gaelic is much higher on the islands (22%) than in Scotland as a whole (just over 1%). Of the island groups with the highest proportions of Gaelic speakers, Scalpay (Harris) had the most with 86.2%. A large number of people in Tiree, Raasay and Skye speak Gaelic but in the Orkney and the Shetland Islands the proportion of Gaelic speakers is lower than for Scotland as a whole.

In 2001, 9.5% of islanders worked in agriculture, hunting, forestry and fishing, compared with 2.4% for Scotland.

Historic Scotland

Historic Scotland looks after over 300 properties – a wealth of ancient monuments and historic buildings and structures. In Scotland, there are more than 52,000 protected ancient monuments and historic buildings, including prehistoric burial tombs, standing stones, castles, churches, great houses, thatched cottages, lighthouses, bridges and industrial buildings. Even although many of them are in private ownership, they are still legally protected.

The prehistoric monuments in the care of Historic Scotland include some of the finest in Europe and it is in the Northern and Western Isles that the prehistoric monuments legacy is exciting, fascinating and has such a variety of interest.

In recognition of their outstanding value, several of the Orkney sites, which date back to 3000–2000 BCE, have been inscribed by UNESCO as The Heart of Neolithic Orkney World Heritage Site. Included in this site is Skara Brae, northern Europe's best preserved Neolithic stone-built village. It is situated in the beautiful Bay of Skaill near the village of Sandwick. It had been buried under the sand for over 4,000 years and was discovered in 1850 when a storm ripped the sand away and ushered the ancient village into the nineteenth-century limelight. Visit it if you can – in the quiet setting, you feel as if you are treading into the past, disturbing the ancestors. The roofless houses, linked by covered passages, have central hearths, stone bed frames and a stone dresser. There is also a paved courtyard where the village council probably met.

Then there is the Maes Howe burial mound, the finest chambered tomb in north-west Europe. It is older than the Egyptian pyramids and was built around 3000 BCE. You have to stoop low to get in and, needless to say, the Vikings have been there before you – having broken in to see what things of value they could find and left inscriptions on the wall. One of the inscriptions, Viking graffiti if you like, hints of them having found treasure.

The Stones of Stenness are a unique and early expression of the ritual customs of Neolithic peoples. There are only four of the original twelve stones left, the tallest being around 19 feet, and they date back to around at least 3000 BCE. There is plenty of speculation on what they are all about – perhaps a sacrificial altar. They are about a mile away from the Ring of Brogar, the finest truly circular late Neolithic or early Bronze Age stone ring. It's a magnificent circle of upright stones with an enclosed ditch spanned by causeways.

Shetland has an intriguing Neolithic complex at Staneydale with a large, heel-shaped hall containing a big oval chamber. Around it are the ruins of houses, walls and cairns of the same period.

On the Shetland island of Mousa, there is the amazingly well-preserved Mousa Broch, the finest surviving Iron Age broch. It is still so intact that you can climb up within its twin walls. The climb will reward you with a magnificent view across the small island.

And, at Jarlshof, you can take a walk from prehistory into history. This is a complex, three-acre site which includes remains from the Bronze Age, the Iron Age, the Pictish era, the Norse era and the Middle Ages. Parts of four wheelhouses date from the Pictish era and there are remains of an entire Viking settlement.

On Lewis, the mysterious stone circle, avenue and alignments at Calanais, dramatically set against mountain and sea, are described by Historic Scotland, who should know a thing or two about ancient monuments, as 'outstanding'. They date from around 2900–2600 BCE.

The following is a table of island properties, managed by Historic Scotland, where admission is paid.

Table 2 Island properties, managed by Historic Scotland, where admission is paid

Site	Number of Visitors in 2002	Description
Skara Brae, Orkney	59,297	A prehistoric village, more than 5,000 years old, with stone-built furniture still visible
Broch of Gurness, Orkney	11,218	The base of the broch sits in the remains of an Iron Age village and there is also a Pictish house
Bishop and Earl's Palaces, Kirkwall, Orkney	8,897	A twelfth-century hall-house with a later splendid Renaissance addition
Brough of Birsay, Orkney	5,971	A Pictish and Norse powerbase, reached by crossing a tidal inlet
Maes Howe, Orkney	3,386	A prehistoric chambered cairn, renowned also for Viking graffiti
Jarlshof, Shetland	9,617	A complex site that includes Iron Age wheelhouses, a Viking long house and Bronze Age ruins
Kisimul Castle, Barra	2,081	The only surviving medieval castle in the Western Isles
Iona Abbey and Nunnery	60,245	A pilgrimage site, associated with St Columba
Rothesay Castle, Bute	10,245	An unusual circular castle that was the favoured home of the Stewart kings
Inchcolm Abbey, Incholm, Firth of Forth	15,058	Best preserved group of monastic buildings in Scotland
Loch Leven Castle	12,373	Situated on an island in Loch Leven, this castle is where Mary, Queen of Scots was imprisoned in 1567, before escaping the following year
Inchmahome Priory, Lake of Menteith	14,588	On an island in the Lake of Menteith, this Augustine monastery was founded in 1238. Robert the Bruce made three visits Mary, Queen of Scots lived there briefly as an infant

Loch Lomond Islands

When you think of Scottish islands, you do not think of Loch Lomond. And when you think of Loch Lomond you do not think of Scottish islands. That could be because, although the dictionary definition of an island is a mass of land surrounded by water, the perception is that it has to be offshore and that the island has to be surrounded by sea water. The General Register Office for Scotland, in its 2001 census of Scottish inhabited islands, says its definition of an island is 'a mass of land surrounded by water, separate from the Scottish mainland. On that basis, out go the Loch Lomond islands – but we'll be keeping them in.

Surprisingly, there are about sixty islands in Loch Lomond but, in this chapter, we'll concentrate on what I would call the fifteen main ones. They have a distinct beauty and fascinating history all of their own that merit their inclusion in any book on the Scottish islands.

With the exception of three of them, all are privately owned. Inchcailloch is owned and managed by Scottish Natural Heritage as part of the National Nature Reserve, while Bucinch and Ceardach are the property of the National Trust for Scotland. Public access to the islands owned by these two organisations is free.

Many of the islands are designated Sites of Special Scientific Interest and are important havens for wildlife. In particular, from April to August, the islands have a large number of ground-nesting birds.

The information on the chosen fifteen Loch Lomond islands has been drawn from loch-lomond.net/islands and incallander.co.uk/islands, carefully compiled by Alistair Reid, and, with thanks, I have permission to take advantage of both.

Bucinch – The Island of Goats

The whole island is densely covered with trees and bushes and has been uninhabited and completely unspoiled for centuries but, on the south-east shore, there are remains of an old stone jetty. On the east bank, there is a memorial to four Clyde shipyard workers who were drowned there during a weekend boating trip last century.

Clairinsh – The Flat Island

According to Alistair Reid, this island is important in local history, for in 1225 the Third Earl of Lennox, the owner of much of the southern part of Loch Lomond, gave the island to his clerk, named Buchanan, who had to pay an annual rent of one pound of wax. This was the first land owned by a Buchanan but the clan grew strong and, until 1682, held much of the east side of Loch Lomond. Clairinsh was bought in 1682 by the Third Duke of Montrose and it remained the property of this family for the next 250 years. The Clan Buchanan still looked on this small island as the birthplace of their grandeur and over the centuries had honoured it by using its name as their battle slogan – 'Clar Innis!'. In 1934, they acquired it for the Buchanan Society and today it is part of the Loch Lomond Nature Reserve.

Eilean Vow – Cow Island

This tiny island contains the remains of a MacFarlane castle that was built to replace the one destroyed by Cromwell on Inveruglas Island (*see below*). It is now overgrown with trees.

Fraoch – Heather Island

This is a small, rocky island with a multitude of plant life. Legend has it that the island was once known as Luss Prison – that is how it was described in a 1792 local authority plan for Dunbartonshire, Loch Lomond and its Environs. And, being so near to Luss on the mainland yet so isolated and secure, it would certainly have been a convenient place to deposit the local undesirables.

Inchcailloch – Island of the Old Woman

That old woman was St Kentigerna who arrived on the island in 717 CE from Ireland with her brother and son and she settled there. This is one of the most accessible of Loch Lomond's islands and was once recognised as being sacred because of its long association with Christianity. In the twelfth century, a church was built and dedicated to the Old Woman's memory and, for the next five centuries, people from the mainland rowed across to worship and to conduct their funerals. Although the church was abandoned in 1670, the graveyard was used until 1947. The remains of farm dwellings can be seen but this livelihood appears to have died out around 1770. The graveyard on the island was used by the Clan MacGregor and on an old gravestone you can see the name of Gregor MacGregor who died in 1623. He was an uncle of Rob Roy. The island can be reached by ferry and it has 20,000 visitors a year. It is owned by Scottish Natural Heritage.

Inchconnachan – Colquhoun's Island

This island boasts a wealth of secluded bays that no other Loch Lomond island can match and, throughout the summer, you can see them filled with overnighting yachts and cruisers. You might also see one of the capercaillies that nest on the island. There is a 1920s wooden bungalow which used to be the holiday home of Lady Arran Colquhoun, sister of Sir Ivan Colquhoun, who was once the holder of a power-boat speed record. She supposedly introduced wallabies to the island. They roam wild and can still be seen occasionally. It is also claimed that, for two centuries, there were illicit whisky stills on the island.

Inchcruin – Round Island

This island is large and mostly wooded. It has several small beaches and is approachable by boat. It has a solitary house, reckoned to be about 200 years old, and it is on the site of an even earlier house. The fields were farmed until the mid nineteenth century and the island is now used as a private holiday retreat.

Inchfad – Long Island

This island is certainly different and goes against the grain, if you see what I mean, as it used to have a whisky distillery that was actually legit and above board. The ruins are still there. The distillery was owned by an ancestor of the family who today run the island mail service and boat yard. A canal was built to minimise the distance the raw materials for the whisky had to be manhandled. There are two houses – a modern bungalow that served as the original farmhouse and a wooden house used as a holiday home.

Inchgalbraith – Island of the Galbraiths

This minuscule island is thought to be a crannog, built by Iron Age man. Crannogs were built as safe dwelling places from attackers or predators and in mediaeval times this crannog was strong enough to support the castle of the Galbraiths. The castle is now in ruins but can be seen through the trees – in fact, the ruins occupy most of the island.

Inchlonaig – The Yew Tree Island

Quite a gem – this island has traces of man dating back to 5000 BCE. Dark green yew trees are scattered across the island – King Robert the Bruce first planted these ancient trees in the fourteenth century to supply bows for his archers at the Battle of Bannockburn. That's one version. The other is that he used the trees that were already there and later replaced them. In more recent times the island was used as a deer park and its stone-built cottage, now used as a holiday home, once provided shelter for drunks seeking a cure for their alcoholism.

Inchmoan – Peat Island

For centuries Inchmoan was a source of peat fuel for Luss. Nature has taken over the centre of the island – it has been described as a jungle of plant life, with pear, rhododendron, birch, alder, gorse, bog myrtle and blueberry. The north and south shores offer long, curving sandy beaches and the western peninsula is covered in Scots pine trees and has a large, two-storey ruined building. The neighbouring island of Inchcruin can almost be touched from the eastern tip of Inchmoan and the narrow passage between the two islands is known as The Geggles.

Inchmurrin – St Murrin's Island

This island is the largest on Loch Lomond and is steeped in history, having been visited by Saint Mirren (after whom the island is named), Robert the Bruce and Mary Queen of Scots. The ruins of a seventh century monastery and the Lennox Castle can still be seen. It was to this castle that the Earl of Lennox and his family retreated from Balloch in order to escape the plague. Isabella, Countess of Albany, was exiled here after all her male relatives were given the chop in Stirling in the fifteenth century. At the last count there were ten residents plus one horse, one dog, a herd of beef cattle, a few goats and a number of pheasants.

Inchvannach – The Island of Monks

A large house has stood on the site of an old monastery since 1760. The peak of the island is called Tom na Clag – Hill of the Bell. It is here that the monks rang the bell as the call of prayer.

Inveruglas – Island of the Black Stream

The black stream enters the loch at the village of Inveruglas on the mainland. The island's trees hide the ruins of the Clan Macfarlane's castle in the east. The castle was sacked by Oliver Cromwell in the seventeenth century.

Tarbet Isle – Isle of the Portage

According to Alistair Reid, the name 'Tarbet' comes from the

Viking word for 'portage', a place where boats (longboats in this case) could be dragged or carried over a narrow strip of land. The portage in this case is the narrow strip of land between the north end of Loch long and Loch Lomond, where the Viking King Haakon's men used the portage for bringing their longboats to create havoc among the communities of Loch Lomond. Justice, however, was on its way – when sailing to re-join the fleet of Haakon they lost ten ships in a storm on Loch Fyne and were then destroyed at the Battle of Largs.

St Kilda

St Kilda is fascinating, mysterious and, like so many of the islands, steeped in history but, in itself, it is not an island. It is, in fact, the name for a cluster of islands forty-one miles west of Benbecula and it is the largest island group in what is known as the Atlantic Outliers. What is generally regarded as the island of St Kilda is Hirta, the archipelago's main island, and archaeologists believe there is evidence of human occupation as far back as the Iron Age with the remains of a pottery and earth house. Occupation on St Kilda has always been difficult and harsh. They were often cut off by storms and by the world at large. Its isolation and individuality had seemed stirring and inspiring to those who lived elsewhere but the itchy feet of the youngsters, realising there was a different world out there, plus health, tourism and general hardship all impacted on the islanders. The last thirty-six inhabitants, all Gaelic speakers, of Hirta were evacuated at their own request in 1930, ending several years of harsh existence. The Marquis of Bute bought the island in 1934 and in 1956 bequeathed it to the National Trust for Scotland.

Being in comparative isolation in the Atlantic fifty miles to the West of the Outer Hebrides did not leave it unscathed in wartime. In 1912, a wireless transmitter was installed on the island by the government and this resulted in a German submarine shelling the island during the First World War. The church was damaged and a store destroyed but no one was hurt and the submarine was later captured by an armed trawler. In 1957, the Ministry of Defence erected masts and radar domes on the peak of the volcanic rock on the island and established a base there. It is used as a radar tracking station for the missile range on Benbecula. In addition to the mast sites on top of the hill, the Ministry of Defence has developed and now occupies 34,025 square feet of buildings within the village and they also house a National Trust Working

Party. The Ministry has just renewed its lease for twenty-five years at a rental of £100,000 a year – that is what you call commitment and what the landlord, the National Trust for Scotland, calls a good deal. In 1986, St Kilda was designated by UNESCO as Scotland's first World Heritage Site and is seen as a candidate for Double World Heritage status.

It's not easy to get there – you need to get permission from the National Trust for Scotland – and weather conditions frequently make it difficult to land there. Nonetheless, around 2,500 visitors manage it each year. When they do get the chance, some of the island's keenest visitors are climbers. The Mountaineering Council of Scotland regard St Kilda as being the birthplace of Scottish climbing and say there is compelling recorded evidence that the first recreational climbing in the UK went on there. Charles Barrington, who made the first ascent of the Eiger, visited St Kilda in 1883 to see what could be learned from the climbing methods of the islanders and many leading climbers have since followed suit.

Historic Scotland has put together what it rightly calls some fascinating facts about St Kilda and they are worthy of your perusal:

- St Kilda is home to Europe's most important sea bird colony and it is one of the major seabird-breeding stations in the North Atlantic
- It has the world's largest colony of gannets' nests
- It has the largest colony of fulmars in the British Isles
- Stac an Armin (191 metres) and Stac Lee (165 metres) are the highest sea stacks in Britain
- Two kinds of mice (the St Kilda house mouse and the St Kilda field mouse) used to be found on St Kilda. Both were larger varieties of the mainland house mouse and wood mouse respectively. They were probably brought to St Kilda by Norsemen. The house mouse became extinct when the islanders left in 1930

- The St Kilda wren is a larger sub-species of the mainland wren and is found throughout the St Kilda archipelago
- In the 1850s, forty-two islanders left to emigrate to Australia. Many of them died en route but a few settled in Melbourne and, to this day, a suburb of the city is called St Kilda. There is also a St Kilda in New Zealand
- In 1726, a St Kildan visited Harris, caught smallpox there and died from it. His clothes were returned to St Kilda in 1727 and they brought the disease with them. Most of the islanders died – only one adult and eighteen children survived the outbreak on Hirta. The owner of St Kilda had to send people from Harris to repopulate the island
- In 1840, what is believed to have been the last great auk recorded in the British Isles was killed by St Kilda islanders. It is said they thought it had caused a violent storm and they suspected it was a witch. Four years later the last great auks in the world were killed in Iceland
- Seabirds formed a major part of the St Kildan diet, especially gannets, fulmars and puffins. At one time, it was estimated that each person on St Kilda ate 115 fulmars every year.

Orkney and Shetland

For years, Orkney and Shetland have been given a raw deal by cartographers. They are those wee bits that should be at the top of the map of the UK but which tend to be stuck in a space at the side – or wherever they can be fitted in. They either end up in a spot which is of no real geographical relevance to where the islands really are or they might just be left out altogether – but not in this literal map. The Orkney and Shetland story is so important and different that it merits this separate chapter.

Between them, Orkney and Shetland have more than 170 islands, so you could island hop there forever. Tourism is an important and growing part of the Shetland and Orkney economies but the islands have been receiving visitors for centuries – although not all of them were welcome – and that is part of the absorbing history which keeps the tills ringing today.

Orkney and Shetland share much of their history, having been colonised by Norsemen who imposed their own culture, language and customs. Norse settlers began arriving around 900 CE. By the late ninth century, Shetland and Orkney were firmly under Norse control. Orkney was ruled by Norwegian kings under a semi-autonomous earldom while Shetland was ruled directly from Norway for nearly 300 years from 1195 and was part of a Norse empire which brought together Sweden, Denmark and Norway. Shetland is just under twice the size of Orkney yet has six times as much coastline. There is no shortage of seabirds on both groups of islands. Shetland has a considerable population of seals and is probably the best place in the whole of Europe to see an otter. Their comparative isolation has created their individuality but it has also made them the stepping stone for explorers, navigators, warmongers and settlers who have all left their mark over the centuries.

Orkney is closer to Oslo than to London. Lerwick, the

Shetland capital, is closer to Bergen than it is to Aberdeen. When they talk about 'the mainland' in Orkney or Shetland, they do not mean the rest of Scotland but mainland Orkney or Shetland. Scotland is 'the south' – the only other place where I have encountered this type of island humour was in Tasmania where they would describe Australia as 'that island to the north'.

Ancient monuments from the Norse age abound in Orkney and Shetland. They are well-preserved and looked after for the benefit of the tourists as well as the community and our heritage but people have lived on these islands for over 5,000 years from Neolithic times and the ancient houses, burial chambers, standing stones, brochs and early chapels are there to tell the tale. The Mousa Broch, for example, just off the east coast of mainland Shetland, is the finest and best preserved of all of Scotland's ruined Iron Age brochs and it is one of Shetland's main archaeological treasures. It was built between the first and second centuries BCE. The archaeological site at Jarlshof spans the ages – there are remains of village settlements from the Bronze Age to the Vikings. These are just two examples of the heritage sites in Shetland which are road maps of an enthralling history for such an isolated and comparatively small place, matched, and perhaps beaten, by Orkney.

Orkney's Skara Brae is my favourite. This is a Stone Age settlement which was buried under the sand for over 4,000 years until it was exposed by a storm in 1850. It is a unique insight into the way of life of prehistoric tribes. It's like strolling through an ancient village – you can see the houses, the beds, the cupboards and tables, all within sight of the beautiful beach which placed it in its unique time warp.

There's so much more to choose from but, as I picked out two from Shetland, I will also offer one more from Orkney – Maes Howe, a huge Stone Age burial cairn dating from around 3000 BCE. You have to stoop low to get into the central chamber of what has been described as one of the supreme achievements of prehistoric Europe but it is well worth that stoop.

When Maes Howe was opened up in 1851, it was found that generations of grave robbers had already been there – and, inevitably, they included the Vikings, who left behind what must be some of the first examples of graffiti. That's when you find that Maes Howe stooping started a long time ago. One Viking inscription states, 'Many a beautiful woman has stooped in here, however pompous she might be.' Another perhaps says it all about the Vikings – 'Thor and I bedded Helga.'

Orkney played an important part in both the First and Second World Wars mainly because of Scapa Flow, the seaway running between the mainland of Orkney and Hoy. For the first half of the twentieth century, it was the main base for the Royal Navy. The entire German fleet – seventy-four ships in all – was interned here after the First World War and scuttled by their commanding officer. In the Second World War, despite what was believed to be considerable coastal defences, a German U-boat got through to Scapa Flow to torpedo *HMS Royal Oak*. A total of 833 perished and the wreck is still there as an official war grave. It was after that that Churchill ordered the building of the Churchill Barriers to seal off the eastern approaches to Scapa Flow, a £2.5 million job which was a lot of money at the time. Many wrecks are still there to be seen and you can motor down the Barriers on your way to Lamb Holm, the site of the Italian Chapel. In 1943, Italian prisoners-of-war built the little chapel out of Nissen huts, scrap metal, driftwood and concrete.

In ancient times, the Shetland capital was Scalloway which is dominated by the ruins of a seventeenth-century castle. Its harbour was the headquarters for the boats that made regular trips to occupied Norway to rescue refugees during the Second World War. In fact, these mercy missions were so regular that they acquired the name 'Shetland Bus'.

Lerwick, Shetland's capital, is Britain's most northerly town. It began as a temporary settlement in the seventeenth century, with the Dutch herring fleet its main customers, and, in that century, it too was an important base for the Royal Navy. It developed into a major fishing port and it figured prominently in the oil boom of the 1970s.

Kirkwall is the Orkney capital. It is the home of St Magnus's Cathedral, built in 1137 by Norse leader Rognwald in memory of his murdered uncle Magnus. Nearby is the seventeenth-century Earl's Palace, built for the second Earl of Orkney, and Tankerness House, a sixteenth-century merchant's home and now a local museum. The public library, founded in 1683, is Scotland's oldest.

I have given you over a thousand words on why Orkney and Shetland, although part of Scotland, are so different in their way of life. Here are two more examples, both of them from Shetland. The small Shetland island of Skerries has a population of about seventy and two brothers of secondary-school age. They go to the Skerries Secondary School – Scotland's smallest secondary school and the only two-pupil secondary school in Britain. There are threats to close it but so far the parents are winning.

Another school story. The rugby team at Anderson High School in Lerwick last year drew an away game against Millburn Academy in Inverness in the Bell Lawrie White Scottish Cup. To play that tie, they had to set off on the Monday night, play the game on the Tuesday afternoon and get back to Shetland for school on the Wednesday. Three days to play a game of rugby, but that typifies what life is like on Shetland and Orkney – they lie apart and like it that way but they are also part of Scotland.

Shorts

The Welsh undoubtedly hold the record for having the longest place names in Britain but when it comes to shorts the Scottish islands are in the top three in the UK.

There are three places in the UK with names which take up only two letters and they are all in Scotland. (Norway and Nebraska, by the way, have the shortest names in the world – Norway has a town called A and Nebraska comes next alphabetically with a town called B).

Britain's shortest three are Ae, which is in Dumfries and Galloway, Bu, in Orkney and Oa on Islay.

Bu is on the small Orkney island of Wyre and Bu is Norse for 'cattle'. Wyre, like most of Orkney and Shetland, has a strong Viking history and Viking names on farms and islands abound.

The place in history for Oa (pronounced the same as 'oh') on Islay is more recent and tragic. In October 1918, during the last few weeks of the First World War, there occurred one of the worst naval disasters of that war when the armed mercantile cruiser *Otranto* was in collision with the steamer *Kashmir*, eight miles off the coast of Ireland. Both were carrying United States troops and, while the *Kashmir* was able to limp to Greenock with no casualties, the *Otranto* was less fortunate. A British destroyer, in terrible conditions and with great heroism, managed to take more than 350 men off the *Kashmir*, but the *Otranto* continued to drift in heavy seas and was smashed on rocks off the coast of Islay. In all, 434 men lost their lives and only sixteen managed to make it to the safety of the Islay shore. Most of the dead were buried on Islay before being transferred to the USA.

In February that year, there was another naval disaster involving American troops. This time it was the *Tuscania*, a luxury ocean liner which had been requisitioned by the British government for war service. It was carrying American troops to

Europe for combat when it was hit by a German torpedo off the coast of Ireland. The rescuers did well – of the 2,235 men on board only 166 of them perished.

Oa overlooks the scene of this disaster and it is here that America erected a monument, in the name of President Woodrow Wilson, to the memory of the 600 men of the *Otranto* and *Tuscania* who died within sight of Oa.

Years ago, when on a visit to Islay, I met James Roberts. His father, David, at the age of seventeen, had been one of the sixteen *Otranto* men who made it to the safety of Islay and to the comfort and hospitality generously given by the Islay people. In 1970, at the age of sixty-nine, David Roberts paid a return visit to Islay on a nostalgic visit and to give his thanks to the people of Islay who had been so kind to him after what must have been a terrible ordeal for a seventeen-year-old. There were still locals there to remember him when he went back in 1970.

When I met James Roberts in 1987, he had been determined for years to visit the spot where his father staggered ashore. He told me, 'I feel it has been a sort of pilgrimage for me. It was remarkable that my father was able to survive the tragedy. He couldn't get over how well the people treated him.' To get to that monument to 600 men, James Roberts had to leave his car and take an hour-and-a-half trek across a moor. He admits he cried and prayed while there as he paid tribute to the memory and salvation of his father, for the souls who perished and the bravery and hospitality of those who rescued and cared for the survivors.

The Impostors

The first island I visited was in 1955 when I lived in Dar es Salaam. I was a cub reporter on the *Tanganyika Standard* and was on a fantastic trip to the Rufiji Delta which involved an overnight stop at the island of Mafia, just off the coast of what is now Tanzania. The name has nothing to do with the crime syndicate but it is probably a contraction of a Swahili phrase meaning 'a healthy place to live'. Mafia made history in 1915 when the British used it as the first place in Africa to launch assembled planes for reconnaissance missions. They were after the German light cruiser *The Koenigsberg*, which was creating havoc in that part of the world with the British Navy – and they eventually got it. It has since become a favourite haunt of big game fishermen and scuba divers for whom the record catches and resplendent coral make it a water sports paradise.

This was island number one and I have been hooked on island life ever since but my next journalistic assignment taught me to beware of island impostors – not to be fooled by their name. There are some which call themselves islands and, in some cases, there could be valid historical reasons for this but, with the best will in the world, they are not islands.

I left – temporarily – the East African shores and continued my journalistic career by joining the *Galloway Gazette* in Newton Stewart and, before long, I was sent to cover a story on the Isle of Whithorn. Great, I thought, my first Scottish island but I was too late – by about a couple of centuries. The cause-way which connects it to the mainland had long since been covered by houses and other buildings and it had lost its island status. But not its place in history – it was here that St Ninian founded the first Christian church north of Hadrian's Wall and it was in fact a commemorative event that I was covering for my newspaper.

I stayed with the *Galloway Gazette* for about a year then moved to another newspaper, the now defunct *Fifeshire Advertiser*, and this is when I came across my second impostor island. It was no surprise to me as I knew all about Burntisland – Burntisland Shipyard used to have a football team which played in the Scottish Cup. At the *Fifeshire Advertiser*, it was not long before I was sent to Burntisland to cover a story and it was with Town Council officials and the newspaper's local correspondent that I made my enquiries about the island that was not an island and certainly did not seem to have been burned. It seems that there were around twenty different spellings of the name and one favoured explanation was that the name came from the burning of a few fishermen's huts on a small island where the town now stands. I found that a bit disappointing.

It was a number of years later before I came across my third island impostor, the Black Isle just north of Inverness. My wife and I were motoring north to visit former neighbours, Calum Macdonald and his wife Lorna from North Uist. Calum and his brother Rory were co-founders of the popular Scottish band with firm island roots, Runrig. It was my wife who asked why the Black Isle was not really an island and I could not give her an explanation. It is not an island and it is not black – that was about as much as I could tell her. Since then I have checked out its web site and that tells me that the name could come from an ancient association with witchcraft and the black arts in medieval times. Sorry, Burntisland – that's a lot better than a few fishermen's huts going up in smoke.

Inchbraoch near Montrose in the east of Scotland used to be an island – as recently as the 1991 census. But the 2001 census said that, since 1991, an area between the south of Inchbraoch and the mainland had been reclaimed as land – therefore, Inchbraoch lost its status and became part of the mainland.

Then there is Inchmahome. It is a bit unfair to list this as an impostor because it is, indeed, an island – it meets our criterion of a mass of land surrounded by water – but it is an island with a difference. It is in the middle of the Lake of Menteith, Scotland's only lake. We prefer to call them lochs but it became a lake because of a historic mix-up with the word *laigh*, the Scots for low-lying ground which applied to the whole area.

Folk

Flora MacDonald's Grave on the Isle of Skye

People and Personalities

Anderson, Arthur

Born in Shetland in 1792, he was a ship-owner and philan-thropist. Before he volunteered to serve in the Royal Navy during the Napoleonic Wars, his first job was curing fish. He successfully moved into the shipping business and became chairman of P&O. He founded the first newspaper in Shetland, set up a fish-processing factory and won the Orkney and Shetlands parliamentary seat in 1847. The house where he was born, Bod of Gremista, was restored as a museum by P&O to mark the company's 150th anniversary.

Baikie, William Balfour

Born in Kirkwall, Orkney, in 1825, he was a Royal Navy surgeon. He explored the River Niger in West Africa, penetrating 250 miles further than any explorer, and he translated parts of the Bible and Prayer Book into Hausa. He died when on leave in Sierra Leone in 1864 and has earned his place as one of the most scientific of Scotland's team of nineteenth-century explorers. He is commemorated by a monument in St Magnus Cathedral in Kirkwall.

Blair, Eric

Better known as George Orwell, he went to Jura to complete *Nineteen Eighty-Four* during the summer months from 1946 to 1948. He chose Jura because it was 'an extremely un-getatable place'. He lived in a remote farmhouse called Barnhill and led a Spartan existence. The title of his famous book was arrived at by simply reversing the last two digits of the year in which it was finished.

Cailleach

You don't want to visit her – she is the infamous Celtic storm goddess whose weapon is the renowned whirlpool of

Corrievrechan, between Jura and the uninhabited island of Scarba. The Corrievrechan is one of the world's most spectacular whirlpools and it is thought to be caused by a rocky pinnacle below the sea. There are numerous legends about the place. The Cailleach supposedly decides which ships will sink and which will survive. St Columba is said to have navigated it in full flood, calming the waters with words alone. One boat she did spare had George Orwell on board. Along with three companions (including his three-year-old son Richard), he nearly drowned in the whirlpool during a fishing trip in August 1947. The outboard motor of his vessel was washed away and they had to row to a nearby island and wait for several hours before being rescued by a passing fisherman.

Gow, John

It was not a good day in Eday for Gow who was described as a notoriously inept pirate. He was born in Stromness and, in 1724, he tried to attack Carrick House, the home of Eday's laird, but his vessel ran aground. He then asked the laird for help, was taken prisoner and sent to London, where he was tortured and executed. Sir Walter Scott based his novel *The Pirate* on the hapless Gow.

Horlick, Sir James

Sir James – of that well-known beverage fame – bought Gigha in 1944 and created the famous gardens at Achamore House. He converted some deciduous woodland into one of the finest gardens on the west coast of Scotland. He died at Achamore in 1972, leaving the plants and an endowment for their upkeep to the National Trust for Scotland. It is a place of pilgrimage for plantsmen from all over the world.

Lever, William Hesketh

In 1918, William Lever, founder of the soap empire Unilever, bought Lewis and Harris and spent nearly a million pounds trying to develop the fishing industry. He created Mac-

Fisheries, which owns a chain of retail fish shops. He had great ideas and ambitions for the two islands but fought the islands' centuries-old tradition of crofting, creating a fair amount of local bitterness. He ran out of money and his dreams died with him. His departure left a huge gap in the local economy – and led to mass emigration. He was created Lord Leverhulme.

Livingstone, Neil

He was born in Ulva in 1788 and was the father of the explorer David Livingstone. The failure of the potato crop in the early 1790s led most of the 600 inhabitants of Ulva to leave Scotland for America or Canada but Neil settled for cotton spinning in Blantyre, where David was born. In 1865, eight years before he died in Africa, David made a steamer trip to Iona, Staffa and Mull and visited the ancestral home on Ulva which, by then, was in ruins. It was that year that he learned that his son Robert, a soldier in the Union Army, had been killed in the American Civil War.

MacDonald, Flora

There is no way she could be left out. Born in South Uist, she conveyed Bonnie Prince Charlie, disguised as an Irish servant girl, over the sea to Skye. She was arrested seven days after parting with the prince in Portree and spent a short time in the Tower of London. She went on to marry a local man, had seven children and emigrated to America, where her husband was taken prisoner during the American War of Independence. She returned to Scotland, lived with her brother and was re-united with her husband on his release. They re-settled in Skye where she died at the age of sixty-eight after an eventful life engraved in Scottish history. She died in the same bed as the one that had been occupied by Bonnie Prince Charlie on his way to Portree and by Dr Johnson when he met her on his famous trip with James Boswell.

MacEwen, Sir William

Born in Rothesay, he made his name in antiseptic surgery, which Lister had pioneered. He removed the first brain tumour in 1879 and his bone-grafting technique produced a surgical cure for the effects of the locally endemic disease of rickets.

Mackenzie, Agnes Muriel

Born in Stornoway in 1891, she was a successful and popular writer on Scottish literature and history and a historical novelist despite being handicapped by bad eyesight and poor hearing. Her surviving correspondence and papers, including some manuscript poetry, are in the National Library of Scotland.

Mackenzie, Sir Alexander

An explorer and fur-trader, he was born in Stornoway, Lewis, in 1755. In 1779, he joined the North West Fur Company in Canada and, in 1788, he established Fort Chipewayan on Lake Athabasca. From there he discovered the Mackenzie River, Canada's longest, in 1789. He followed it to its estuary at the Arctic Ocean and, during 1792–93, he became the first European to cross the Rockies to the Pacific. He returned to Scotland via Montreal and published a book about his journey. He was knighted in 1802.

Mackenzie, Colonel Sir Colin

Born in Stornoway in 1755, he comes into the they-don't-make-'em-like-that-any-more category. He served in India, taking part in the third Mysore War, and was instrumental in the capture of Pondicherry in 1793 and of Colombo in 1796. There were heroics galore but he also made his name as a military surveyor and as an expert in all aspects of Indian antiquity. He also worked in Java and Bengal and the Mackenzie Collection of manuscripts, coins, inscriptions and so on is probably the largest hoard of historical material ever amassed.

Mackenzie, Sir Compton

Born in West Hartlepool, the author of *Whisky Galore* and many other novels settled on Barra in 1928. As well as being a prolific and successful writer, he was also a politician. He died in Edinburgh and is buried in Barra.

Maclean, Sorley

This Gaelic poet was born on Raasay. He read English at Edinburgh University (1929–33) and, by the end of the 1930s, he was an established figure on the Scottish literary scene. A teacher and headmaster until his retirement in 1972, his major collection of poems, Reothairt is Contraigh *(Spring Tide and Neap Tide)*, appeared in 1977. Translations of his work from Gaelic (often his own) have been issued in bilingual editions all over the world.

Macmillan, Daniel and Alexander

Daniel was born in Arran in 1813 and Alexander was born there in 1818. In London, the brothers started what was to become the famous book publishing firm. Daniel got out in 1857 when ill health beat him but his two sons eventually joined their Uncle Alexander in the business. One, Frederick, was chairman and the other, Maurice, was a partner. Maurice was the father of former Prime Minister Harold Macmillan.

Macpherson, Sir John

A Skye-born son of a minister, he had a questionable two years as Governor-General of India, lost his next job because of his involvement in some corruption, returned to London on a substantial pension and was then elected to parliament. Accused of bribery, he was fined and lost his seat.

Macquarie, Lachlan

A native of the island of Ulva, he volunteered at the age of fourteen and served with Highland regiments in America, Jamaica, India and Egypt and, in 1809, he became Governor of New South Wales, taking over from Captain Bligh of *Bounty* notoriety. He had a liberal approach and set new standards of paternal government but this did not go down well with all in Australia and at home, and he was recalled in 1820. Nonetheless, he is still regarded as the 'Father of Australia'. His body lies in the Macquarie Mausoleum near Salen in Mull.

McSporran, Seamus

Now retired, he was one of the most celebrated residents on Gigha because he had fourteen jobs on the island. He had the island's only shop, which doubled as a post office, and it was stocked with everything from bananas to televisions. Seamus was also the postman, fireman and petrol-pump attendant. He drove a taxi which also served as the school bus, the ambulance and the hearse. His other duties included pier master, rent collector, registrar of births, marriages and deaths and he also hired bicycles to tourists. He had a uniform or outfit to go with each job. In his spare time, he sold life insurance and was the island undertaker. And he and his wife ran a bed-and-breakfast establishment. In 1989, Seamus was awarded the British Empire Medal for his services to the island. There is, however, one unanswered question – how many pensions did he get?

Martin, Martin

So good they named this Skye author twice. His *Description of the Western Isles in Scotland* was, in 1703, the first published account of life in the Hebrides and it is said that it inspired Boswell and Johnson to make their famous visit to the Highlands and Islands.

Muir, Edwin

Born in Orkney in 1887, he was one of the twentieth century's major poets. He was also a noted critic, translator and autobiographer.

Rae, Dr John

An Arctic explorer with extraordinary stamina, he was born in Stromness with ice in his veins. He was one of the many Orcadians who joined the Hudson's Bay Company, serving as a surgeon in northern Canada. He completed the first survey of Canada's northern coastline.

Robertson, George

A British statesman, he was born on Islay. He studied at Dundee University, became Scottish organiser of the General and Municipal Workers' Union (1969–78) and was elected an MP in 1978. He was Opposition Spokesman on Scotland (1979–80), defence (1980–81) and Foreign and Common-wealth Affairs (1981–83). He then joined the Shadow Cabinet and was spokesman on Scotland (1993–97). He served as Defence Secretary (1997–99) in the Labour government and was appointed Secretary-General of NATO in 1999, stepping down at the end of 2003. He was awarded a peerage in the same year.

Longevity

Fancy living to a ripe old age? A *really* ripe old age? Then head for the Scottish islands. They enjoy life there so much that they cling on to it avidly, aided no doubt by a stress-free lifestyle.

Jura

On Jura, for instance, there is a gravestone in the cemetery at the Chapel of St Earnadail which bears the name of Mary MacGrain, who died in 1856 at the age of 128. One of her ancestors did better than that. Her tombstone inscription says she was a descendant of 'Gilmour MacGrain, who kept One hundred and eighty Christmasses in his own house'.

Lewis

In 2003, the oldest person on Lewis, Catherine Mackenzie, died in a Stornoway residential home at the age of 104. She spent two years in Chicago as a young girl before returning to Lewis. She then trained as a nurse, working in Stornoway until she retired in 1956.

Scalpay

But it is Scalpay, south of Harris, which tops the islands' current longevity league. A *Daily Mail* report in November 2003 said that Christina MacSween, a Scalpay resident, had celebrated her 108th birthday. Her mother died at 100, her cousin Mary – whose birth Christina witnessed as a little girl – had reached 100 and her brother 99, reported the paper. And all were born and raised on Scalpay.

Vikings

The very word itself sends shivers down the spine. The Vikings were the bloodthirsty warriors who raped and pillaged their way through a large part of Scotland, the islands in particular. Words like 'massacre' and 'slaughter' always appear on the same pages as 'the Vikings'. They didn't have the benefit of an Alastair Campbell spin in those days so that more or less sums up the general perception of what the Vikings were and what they did to us.

Kirk Douglas, Tony Curtis and Ernest Borgnine, with the delectable help of Janet Leigh, romanticised it somewhat in the 1958 epic, *The Vikings*, which had two Viking half-brothers quarrelling over the throne of Northumbria. The film certainly got a better press than the Vikings themselves who would seem to have been wrongly represented in our history. Maybe, after all, they were good guys and were beneficent tourists who did not leave death and destruction in their wake. But remember that these were ancient times and life was cheap.

A Shetland Islands tourist brochure sees the Vikings thus: 'Without doubt the greatest abiding influence on Shetland has been the Vikings, who arrived not to rape and pillage but to farm, settle peacefully and raise families.' So who did all this raping and pillaging? Or, more to the point, who were the Vikings? Books on the subject will refer to Vikings on one page, to Norsemen on the next and maybe even Scandinavians somewhere else. One book which is more careful with its choice of words is *The Sea Road: A Viking Voyage Through Scotland*. It was written by Olwyn Owen, Principal Inspector of Ancient Monuments with Historic Scotland and an internationally respected specialist on the Viking period. So I asked her advice on when to use the words 'Vikings' and 'Norsemen' and this is what she told me:

*We have been very lazy about using these words. The strict
meaning of Vikings was people who raided and took shelter.
We should talk about Norsemen in Scotland from the
beginning to the end. Viking has particular connotations. It
is an exciting word. People associate it with rape and pillage
but it is very difficult to sustain that when you look at the
evidence.*

She sees her book as seeking to qualify the barbaric image
of the Vikings in the popular imagination. Here is an extract
that attempts to put the record straight:

*First and foremost the Vikings were travellers. They roamed
far to the east, south and west in their magnificent ships.
Initially they came as raiders and traders but soon they built
links with other civilisations and settled among them.*

*They established towns and a network of communications,
exploited the riches of the East and explored the uncharted
waters of the North Atlantic, colonising uninhabited or
sparsely populated lands on the margins of Europe.*

*And early during this great outpouring of people from the
Scandinavian homelands the Vikings also came to England,
Ireland and Scotland.*

She goes on to state that, from Norway in the ninth century, the Vikings travelled to Orkney and Shetland and established the Orkney earldom as a powerful base from which they
could make inroads into northern and north-east Scotland.
The next landfall was the Western Isles which the Vikings came
to rule just as surely as they did the north and, from there,
their influence was to penetrate into the western part of mainland Scotland.

She adds:

*It was in the north that their influence endured. The Viking
Orkney earldom came to be an important player in the
politics of the emerging nation of Scotland and its influence
was felt into medieval times and beyond. Even today, the*

traveller to Orkney and Shetland enters a Scandinavian Scotland.

Another defence or clarification of the Vikings is made in *Viking Scotland* by Anna Ritchie, who has also set out to address my confusion about the use of Vikings, Norsemen and Scandinavian. This is what she says about the terms:

> *They may appear to be interchangeable but their meanings are different. Viking, in particular, is such an evocative word that it is often used in a general sense to cover the whole episode of raiding and colonising from Scandinavia. In its strict sense, a Viking was a Scandinavian warrior who went out on sea-borne raids.*

So it would seem that the word 'Viking' describes the type of Scandinavian warrior they were, just as some football fans could be described as 'hooligans'. It was not the case of a bunch of travel-hungry Scandinavians with Viking tendencies saying to each other, 'Let's go and raid Scotland.' – Scotland, as such, did not exist when the Vikings first set out in their magnificent ships around the year 800. Then the land that now constitutes Scotland was a mishmash of people who were fighting territorial battles with each other and they were easy pickings for the Vikings. It did not take long for the Northern Isles – Shetland and Orkney – to become a Norwegian colony and, from Orkney, the Scandinavians would eventually take control of large parts of northern Scotland – and more.

The Viking presence in the Northern Isles is traditionally thought to date from around 800 CE until about 1100. But Viking warriors made their first recorded visit to Scotland's coasts in 794 when they were reported by Irish chroniclers to have subjected island after island to 'devastation'. In 795, 'Skye was pillaged' and Iona raided. In 806, sixty-eight Iona monastery monks were slain at a spot that has been known ever since as Martyrs' Bay.

According to Olwyn Owen:

> The traditional end date of the Viking age – about 1100 –
> means absolutely nothing in the Scandinavian areas of
> northern and western Scotland. Twelfth- and thirteenth-
> century Orkney and Shetland, in particular, remained Norse
> in culture. Indeed, the islands remained under the control of
> the Norwegian Crown until 1468.
>
> Even the Western Isles remained subject to Norway until
> 1266. Sometimes we describe the period from about 1100 to
> about 1300 in these areas as 'late Norse'. I prefer not to try
> to fit 'Viking Scotland' into a dating straitjacket, but simply
> to accept that Scandinavian culture became embedded in the
> north and west of the country in the ninth century, developed
> its own momentum and endured as a dominant culture there
> for some 500 years, and its influences still linger today.

Anna Ritchie, in her book, says that Orkney and Shetland
became thoroughly Scandinavian during six centuries of
Norse rule and the ties with Scandinavia have remained strong
through fishing and trade.

Other parts of Scotland were extensively settled by
Norwegians – such as the Western Isles – but, she states, the
intervening centuries have submerged their Scandinavian
character and made them Scottish, their past betrayed only by
the place names coined by their former overlords.

So has history been unkind to them? Anna says in her
book:

> Like all emotive subjects, the Vikings swing between a good
> press and a bad press; even among academics there has been
> a marked cycle in the last few decades in the thinking about
> Viking Scotland, from a view of unremitting bloodshed and
> extermination at the hands of the Vikings to a degree of co-
> existence between the native Pict and Scot and the incoming
> Norsemen.

But she warns that there is a danger of swinging too far and forgetting that the early Viking raiders were committed to outright gain and not to counting human loss. Here's a final quote from her excellent book: 'Scotland has retained a rich memory of this turbulent and long-lasting episode of her past, embodied in language, history and, most of all, in the physical remains of houses, graves, weapons, silverwork and more.'

These remains are manifold, evocative and fascinating. One particular example is Udal Law – the ancient Norse system of inheritance and law. It was brought to Orkney and Shetland by Viking settlers. Udallers have absolute ownership of their land but lack title deeds. In Orkney and Shetland ownership of land extends to the lowest ebb of the spring tide and as far as a stone can be thrown, how far into a river a horse can wade or how far a salmon net can be thrown. Swans are the property of the people in Orkney and Shetland because of Udal Law – elsewhere in the UK they belong to the Crown.

On Skye, The Old Man of Storr, a 165-foot distinctive column of rock shaped like a leaf, presents a real challenge for climbers. In 1891, on the shore below it, a hoard of treasure was unearthed. It was a remarkable collection of silver neck rings, brooches, bracelets and beaten ingots together with tenth-century coins. It is believed they were left there by Norsemen who presumably could not return to claim them. They are now in the antiquity part of the Royal Museum of Scotland in Edinburgh.

On Colonsay, towards the end of the nineteenth century, the grave of a Viking was discovered and, beside his bones, were the remnants of a sword, a knife, an axe, a spear and a shield. But it also contained a set of balances and a number of lead weights. Coins interred with him showed he was from the ninth century – given what accompanied him to his grave, was he a fighter, a trader or both?

It's a question that could probably be asked about all of those Scandinavian invaders.

The
Natural
World

The Skye Terrier

Farm Animals

Sheep

The islands have five distinctive breeds of sheep and they are all descended from the original hardy breeds brought over by the Vikings. They are the Hebridean – also known as St Kilda – the Boreray – also known as the Boreray Blackface – the North Ronaldsay – also known as Orkney – the Soay and the Shetland.

Hebridean

The Hebridean is a two- or four-horned, small, fine-boned, slow-maturing breed which thrives on the poorest of pastures. In 1973, the Rare Breeds Survival Trust identified it as a breed in danger of extinction but the re-introduction of the breed has been incredibly successful. No longer in danger, flocks of Hebrideans are widely spread throughout the UK and Europe. The wool is dense and black and the meat is succulent and low in cholesterol.

Boreray

The Boreray sheep are descendants of a domestic flock left by the St Kildans. They are blackface and Cheviot crosses and have reverted to a wild state. They are now considered a feral breed in their own right.

North Ronaldsay

The North Ronaldsay sheep are something else. They are small, short-tailed, tough and goat-like and they have a variety of colours and horn formations. They also have an unusual eating habit – seaweed. It is an enforced diet. In the mid nineteenth century the island's sheep farmers built a thirteen-mile wall which almost goes round the entire island and keeps the sheep off what little farmland they have. This leaves the sheep with nothing to eat but seaweed, which is plentiful, and they take to it willingly. But, during the lambing period, the ewes are brought inside the dyke to feed on grass for three to four months. In 1993, the wall was breached by the storms that wrecked the oil tanker *Braer* and there was no shortage of volunteers to help re-build it. When the clipping and dipping season begins, the sheep are herded off the beach into a series of drystone 'punds' – the act of punding is perhaps one of the last remaining elements of communal farming in Orkney. The flesh of the North Ronaldsay sheep is iodine rich and gamey and sells well in up-market London restaurants. The sheep are placid and do not seem to object to the enforced diet and the punding. Just as well – there are around two thousand of them and only about sixty islanders.

Soay

The Soay sheep – Soay is part of the St Kilda group of islands – are prehistoric husbandry on four legs. They are the most primitive of all European domestic sheep breeds and have changed little since sheep were first farmed in Britain nearly 4,000 years ago. Some have left the island. Their coloured fleeces are sought after for many craft uses and their carcasses produce lean meat said to be of a delicious flavour and fetching premium prices from the gourmet trade. But not all the sheep that left the island were destined for the kitchen table. In Victorian times, many were taken to become part of ornamental flocks on estates, like Woburn Abbey in Bedfordshire. However, catching them must have been a difficult task. They are small and robust animals with what has been described as a quirky behaviour – meaning that, when they are approached, they scatter individually and at some considerable speed. They can't be rounded up with the help of a sheepdog because they will not group together when threatened; so they have to be cornered, one at a·time, or chased until exhausted. Nothing really quirky about that – it's called survival and they have been doing it for thousands of years. The North Ronaldsay sheep show similar traits.

Shetland

The Shetland sheep, probably brought to the island by the Vikings, have different colours of wool which were used for knitted shawls of fine quality and other items made in the late eighteenth and early nineteenth centuries by wives of men who had been press-ganged into the Royal Navy or whaling in the Arctic. They are short-tailed and are one of the smallest of British breeds.

Cattle

Shetland, which has its own breeds of dog, sheep and pony, is the only Scottish island to have its own breed of cattle.

Shetland

The Shetland was a distinct breed in the Shetlands hundreds of years ago and it appears to have changed very little in that time. The Shetland cow is well known for its ability to produce excellent milk, rich in butterfat. They are very hardy, living well on poor grazing and making good use of roughage. And, of course, their origin is probably Scandinavian.

Sometimes I think we have been sold short by the Scandinavians. They have left us plenty of things that have lasted through hundreds of years and added so much to our culture and spread of life. But sheep and cattle? Why couldn't they have given us some decent footballers and rugby players?

Dogs

There are twelve breeds of dogs which are recognised by the Kennel Club as Scottish breeds and two of them are most definitely from the islands – the Skye Terrier and the Shetland Sheepdog.

Skye Terrier

Various theories have been put forward as to the true origin of the Skye Terrier. One goes that it developed from dogs of a Maltese breed that was brought ashore by sailors, from a wrecked ship of the Spanish Armada, and they mated with indigenous terriers.

According to the Skye Terrier Club, Skye Terriers were known as such approximately 300 years ago and were kept in great numbers on Colonsay as well as Skye. The Club says that Queen Victoria was a keen fancier of the Skye and so adaptable was the dog that it filled the position of being a lady's companion. Its exalted status is summed up by the fact that it was said in Victorian times that 'no Duchess would care to be seen out walking without her Skye Terrier'.

Skye Terriers have competed in dog shows since they were started around 1860. The Skye Terrier of today is mainly a companion and family dog. He is much larger than his ancestors but has lost none of the pluck and sporting instincts of his ancestors. Above all he is renowned for his great loyalty as epitomised so well by the most famous Skye Terrier of them all, Greyfriars Bobby. Many other stories have been told of owners having been parted from their Skyes for a long number of years. The dogs, remembering their masters instantly on their return, took their place at their side as if they had never been parted. All made for Hollywood.

Shetland Sheepdog

The Norse invaders brought with them what some believe were the ancestors of the Shetland sheepdog. Another view is that they might have originated from Greenland Yakkis and Icelandic dogs brought by whalers to Shetland centuries ago. They also have traits and some characteristics of the Swedish Vallhund. There is still more that went into the mix that created this small, highly intelligent dog that is capable of herding with little or no supervision and, indeed, can act as a supervisor because years ago they were used as babysitters.

The islands' harsh climate required a hardy, small dog with a thick, weather-resistant coat. When Shetland became part of Scotland in the fifteenth century, it began importing sheep from the mainland and the Scottish collie, then slightly smaller than today's breed, was crossed with the already-mixed Shetland dogs to give the island breed a more distinct collie-like appearance. The result is the Shetland sheepdog. It is regarded as a popular companion and a useful working dog and it also excels at all events requiring intelligence and agility.

Ponies

The Eriskay Pony

Eriskay ponies have a tough life – and it has always been that way. They are the last surviving remnants of the original native ponies of the Western Isles and they now face the toughest challenge of all – survival.

They are listed by the Rare Breeds Survival trust as Category 1 and that means 'critical'. Catriona Cochrane, who does PR and marketing for the Eriskay Pony Society, a registered charity which exists to protect and promote the ponies, says it is an uphill struggle. She adds, 'Although I would say that the future of the Eriskay is bright, these ponies are still more rare than a giant panda but numbers have risen steadily and now there are around 300 Eriskays in the world.'

These ponies go back a long way. They have ancient Celtic and Norse connections and Eriskays have been proven by measurement to be of similar proportions to those found on ancient Pictish stones in the North and West of Scotland.

Until the middle of the nineteenth century, ponies of the Western Isles type were found throughout the islands and were used as crofters' ponies, undertaking everyday tasks such as bringing home peat and seaweed in basketwork creels slung over their backs, pulling carts, harrowing and even taking children to school.

At one time, many of the Western Isles had their own isolated population of ponies, each of which had evolved its own characteristics due to isolation and selective breeding. But, in the eighteenth and nineteenth centuries, there was a demand for larger working ponies so bigger stallions were introduced to bolster the stock. That did the trick but it also meant that many of the individual characteristics of the island ponies were bred out. But this did not happen in Eriskay because the geography and isolation of the island made it impossible to import stallions. That protected the purity of the breed – but also threatened its future.

Then there emerged an Eriskay pony hero by the name of Eric. Catriona Cochrane tells the delightful story of what she calls 'The Missing Percentages'. While the Eriskay ponies remained unsullied by larger outsiders their numbers dwindled and, by the early 1970s, there were only twenty pure Eriskay mares left on Eriskay – survivors of the original Western Isles pony which had lost its original form on many other islands. But the last known pure stallion on the island died in 1971 so the race to save the pony from extinction was on. This meant bringing in stallions of the Western Isles type – they found one on Rum and one in Stirlingshire. They were as close as you could get to the real Eriskay but using them as studs would mean diluting the purity of the Eriskay Breed. Catriona goes on to say:

> Then, in 1973, to everyone's delight, a previously unrecognised pure Eriskay stallion, Eric, was located on the neighbouring island of South Uist. His owner had gone to great lengths to ensure that he was kept entire, resisting pressure to have him gelded. It is from Eric that all 100% pure animals will be descended.

So Eric has been a busy chap. The progeny of stock sired by Western Isles stallions, although being true to type, were designated 50% pure but through breeding up with the progeny of Eric it has been possible to steadily increase the purity of young stock every generation.

The purity of the breed has gone up from 94% in recent years. It is approaching 97% and the Society is confident that the next generation will be 99% pure.

A superb island story and three cheers for Eric.

The Shetland Pony

No Eric was needed by the only other breed of pony indigenous to the islands – the Shetland pony. Like the Eriskay, it is a breed which has been around for a long time but, unlike the Eriskay, it has prospered and you can find them all over the world.

Whereas Eriskay devotees count each and every pony carefully, a Shetland pony count is difficult. I asked Mrs E. Ward, secretary and treasurer of the Shetland Pony Stud Book Society, how many Shetlands are around and she replied:

> It is very difficult even to hazard a guess. A long time ago the figure that was bandied about was about 60,000 worldwide but I don't think that is realistic at all – in the UK alone we register 2,500 a year and they live till they are about thirty years old.

The Society, formed in 1890, lays down the procedures for the licensing of Shetland stallions and keeps its eye on registrations worldwide – which is quite a task, given that there are what they call 'Daughter Societies' in Australia, Austria, Belgium, Denmark, Finland, France, Germany, the Netherlands, Norway, Poland, Sweden and Switzerland.

The Shetland, with pit pony supreme on its CV, is a tough wee beastie. It is reckoned that, pound for pound, it is the strongest equine known. It can take nine stone or even more on its back – not bad for a little 'un.

Bird Reserves

The Royal Society for the Protection of Birds (RSPB) has over 150 nature reserves throughout the UK, covering more than 240,000 acres. The habitats in Scotland are often on a grander scale than in other parts of the UK. For sheer numbers of birds, the nature reserves on the Scottish islands are special and they are home to the rarest of breeding birds. Here's a bird's-eye islands view, reproduced here with the kind permission of the RSPB:

Coll

This reserve has long, white shell-sand beaches, sand dunes and machair grassland, all typical Hebridean habitats. The reserve is a stronghold for the rare corncrake. The RSPB is managing the reserve with local farmers to help corncrake numbers recover. There are also many other breeding birds on the reserve, including redshanks, lapwings and snipe. In the winter, large numbers of barnacle and Greenland white-fronted geese use the site.

Islay

Loch Gruinart

During the spring there are hundreds of breeding wading birds such as lapwings, redshanks and snipe and the nights resound to the call of the corncrake. Hen harriers nest on the moor and golden eagles and peregrines are there all year round. Loch Gruinart is famous for the large numbers of barnacle and white-fronted geese who spend the winter on Islay.

Upper Killeyan

From the coast you can see choughs, seabirds and occasional golden eagles. Greenland white-fronted geese use the bog and twites can be seen on farmland.

Orkney

Birsay Moors

In the summer, hen harriers, short-eared owls and Arctic skuas nest on the moorland. The Orkney vole is also common on this reserve.

Brodgar

A comparatively new reserve, this one is next to the Neolithic monument of the Ring of Brodgar in the heart of Orkney. You can hear the bubbling curlews and drumming snipe in the summer, along with lapwings, dunlins, redshanks and oyster-catchers. Wildfowl also abound on this small reserve. Shoveller ducks, teals, wigeons, mallards and gadwalls breed nearby and many more species can be seen from the shores of the surrounding lochs.

Cottascarth and Rendall

These are great places to see hen harriers, merlins and short-eared owls. Rendall Moss has one of the highest densities of breeding curlews in Europe.

Hobbister

This reserve is a mixture of moorland, sandflats, saltmarsh and sea cliffs. Hen harriers, short-eared owls and red-throated divers breed on the moorland. On the coast, you can see red-breasted mergansers and black guillemots.

Hoy

The famous Old Man of Hoy rock stack can look down on great skuas, red grouse, dunlins and golden plovers. Seabirds, including guillemots, razorbills and kittiwakes, breed on the cliffs.

Mill Dam, Shapinsay

In the winter, whooper swans can often be seen on this reserve, along with greylag geese. In the summer pintails breed on the marsh along with other ducks, including wigeons and shovellers.

Marwick Head

Thousands of pairs of seabirds crowd on to the cliffs here and the cliff top has spectacular displays of sea campion, thrift and spring squill.

North Hill, Papa Westray

The low cliffs here are home to breeding seabirds, including guillemots, razorbills and kittiwakes. On the hill, a large colony of Arctic terns nests close to Arctic skuas, eiders, ringed plovers and oystercatchers. This is, in fact, the largest ternery in Europe and the reserve also has one of the largest breeding colonies in Britain of black guillemot. It has been described as a wonderland for birdwatchers.

Noup Cliffs, Westray

This is where you can see one of the UK's largest seabird colonies – more than 44,500 guillemots and 12,700 pairs of kittiwakes breed here, along with razorbills and fulmars.

Onziebust, Egilsay

Acquired by the RSPB in 1996, this reserve offers a wonderful array of breeding birds. It has ideal conditions for corncrakes when they arrive from Africa in the spring.

The Loons

This marshland reserve is one of the best remaining marshes in the Orkney Islands. In the summer, pintails and wading birds breed while, in the winter, the flooded marsh attracts hundreds of ducks and a smaller number of white-fronted geese.

Trumland

Red-throated divers, merlins and hen harriers all breed on the heather moorland of this reserve.

Shetland

Fetlar

During the summer, a wealth of birds breed on Fetlar, including 90% of the British population of red-necked phalaropes. These fascinating wading birds can be seen from the RSPB hide or at the Loch of Funzie. Red-throated divers, whimbrels and Arctic and great skuas also breed here.

Loch of Spiggie

This large shallow loch attracts large numbers of wildfowl during the autumn and winter, including whooper swans, wigeons and teals. In the summer, Arctic terns, Arctic and great skuas and kittiwakes can be seen bathing in the loch.

Mousa

Mousa is famous for its 2,000-year-old Iron-Age broch, the best-preserved broch in the world, and it is here that many of the island's 6,000 pairs of storm petrels nest. Mousa also has 400 breeding seals and is home to Arctic terns, black guillemots, Arctic and great skuas, ringed plovers, oystercatchers and a few puffins. The ferry trip to Mousa can offer occasional sightings of porpoises, orca and minke whales.

Sumburgh Head

The cliffs around Sumburgh Head attract thousands of breeding seabirds, including puffins, guillemots, shags and fulmars. Gannets are regularly seen offshore and sometimes you can even spot whales and dolphins.

North Uist

Balranald

Sandy beaches and a rocky foreshore are separated from the machair and marshes by sand dunes and there are also shallow lochs. Many species of birds, including the rare corncrake, nest on the flower-rich machair and croftland.

Ailsa Craig

This privately owned island has one of the largest gannet colonies in the world, with more than 70,000 birds, and is designated as a European Special Protection Area. In addition to the gannet, there are other breeding seabirds including the guillemot, razorbill and small numbers of puffin. Ailsa Craig has at last managed to rid itself of its rat problem – which goes back to 1889 when the first rat was seen on the island at the time of the construction of a new lighthouse. It was thought to have escaped from ships bringing coal or it could have escaped from any one of the many ships wrecked on the rocks before the lighthouse was built. The rats soon multiplied. Their appetite substantially reduced several seabird populations on the island and stopped the puffins breeding for over fifty years. But a University of Glasgow project got rid of the rats by 1992 and the puffins started breeding again.

Long Craig

This is a small island off North Queensferry under the Forth Road Bridge. It has just been given the highest protection under European law to ensure the survival of a rare seabird, the roseate tern. There are only an estimated 660 pairs of roseate terns in Europe and Long Craig regularly supports around 13% of the British breeding population. There were 500 pairs of roseate terns nesting in the Firth of Forth in the last century – in 2003 there were only eight.

Trees

Donald Rodger is a treeman. He operates from his home in Gullane, East Lothian, and travels up and down the country giving advice to local authorities, companies and professional organisations about how to look after trees. In his spare time, he has co-authored a book – and the subject is, of course, trees. It features the hundred most special trees in Scotland – the oldest, the tallest, the rarest and so on – and it has been such a success that he might follow it up with a similar book covering the whole of the UK.

When I met him, I was keen to talk about the trees on the Scottish islands that had made his top one hundred and I was surprised to find that there were only three. He admits that he was also a bit surprised but, of course, this makes those three all the more distinctive.

I recall the story of a bachelor from the south of England being posted to Orkney and being a bit concerned about the social life there. He was told by his colleagues who had been there that he would have a great time in Orkney because there was a girl behind every tree. When he got there he found that there were no trees in Orkney. Well, not quite. There is certainly at least one tree and it has made it into the top one hundred list of Donald Rodger who was kind enough to give me permission to reproduce his information and comments about the three island trees.

The Big Tree of Orkney

Orkney's biggest and oldest tree stands in Kirkwall's Main Street. As well as being a local landmark, the solitary sycamore is known as The Big Tree because Orkney's windswept environment means that few trees can survive or grow to any appreciable size. It appears to have arisen as a windblown seedling and is now several centuries old. Urban development has encroached heavily on the tree which is displaying symptoms of decline. The hollow trunk has been heavily cut back to a stump of about 3 metres (10 feet). However, the tree is clearly a great survivor and new, healthy growth has sprouted from the cut stump.

The Arran Whitebeams

The Isle of Arran is home to two species of tree which do not occur anywhere else in the world – the Arran whitebeam and the Arran cut-leaved whitebeam. They are also Scotland's rarest native trees and, in global terms, are officially classed as dangerously close to extinction. Only a few hundred trees of each species exist, clinging perilously to the steep rocky slopes of two remote glens at the north of the island. The Arran whitebeam was first recorded in 1897 and it is thought to have arisen as a natural hybrid between the rock whitebeam and the ubiquitous rowan. The other rare hybrid, the Arran cut-leaved whitebeam, was first noted in 1952. This appears to have arisen from the Arran whitebeam back-crossing with the rowan. Both species were abundant in the past but have been forced to retreat to their restricted enclaves as the island was progressively improved for agriculture. Small, windswept and stunted, these uniquely Scottish trees are under constant threat from the strong gales and heavy snow storms common in their montane habitat, because the fragile root systems are easily dislodged from the rocky soil.

Inchmahome Veterans

The thirteenth-century priory of Inchmahome, once home to a small community of Augustinian canons, nestles on a small, low-lying island in the middle of the Lake of Menteith. Of the many fine trees on the island, the three veteran sweet chestnuts steal the show in terms of antiquity and character. These heavily gnarled individuals are probably more than 400 years old. Although extensively decayed and hollow, they are still very much alive and are the island's oldest living residents. The girth of their gnarled trunks ranges from 4.36 metres (14 feet

4 inches) to 6 metres (19 feet 8 inches). The largest of the three is known as the Antlered Chestnut because the stag-headed branch resembles the antlers of a deer. The tree might well have been around when Mary, Queen of Scots paid a visit to the island in 1547. Accompanied by her mother, Mary of Guise, the four-year-old infant queen sought refuge at the priory for three weeks following the English victory at the Battle of Pinkie.

Munros

A Munro is a distinct mountain in Scotland that is over 3,000 feet high. The classification is named after Sir Hugh Munro, founder member of the Scottish Mountaineering Club, who, in 1891, published *Munro's Tables*, a list of all the hills which he considered to be over 3,000 feet in height. His original list contained 283 but more modern cartographical techniques have meant that it is possible to measure geographical heights far more accurately than in Munro's day and the last revision, in 1984, added one more to the original total.

Climbing the Munros – Munro-bagging as it is called – is an addictive sport played by thousands of eager climbers and walkers each year. At the last count over 2,000 people had bagged all the Munros – the Scottish Mountaineering Club keeps a list of all those who have bagged the 284 and some have bagged the complete set several times.

The most recent was retired vet Robert Waterston, who bagged his first one when he was eleven – and he climbed the 284th at the age of eighty.

However, if you want to bag the island Munros it is not a major task. There are only thirteen of them and twelve are in Skye. The only other island boasting a Munro is Mull.

The following table lists them.

Table 3 The island Munros

Skye

Name	Translation	Comment
Bruach na Frithe	'Slope of the Deer Forest'	This is a good one for beginners as it's reckoned to be one of the easier Munros, with a comfortable path to the top.
Sgurr Alasdair	'Alexander's Peak'	This is the highest peak on Skye, rising to 3,255 ft, and it is named in Gaelic after the Skye man, Sheriff Alexander Nicholson, who was one of the earliest explorers of the Cuillin (the Skye mountain group). In 1873, he made the first recorded ascent of the peak that bears his name.
Sgurr Dearg	'The Inaccessible Pinnacle'	This is the only Skye Munro that requires rock-climbing ability. Care and experience are needed. Its inaccessible pinnacle, the highest summit in the Cuillin, is said to be the most difficult of all Munro summits and has been the downfall of many a would-be bagger.
Sgurr a' Ghreadaidh	'Peak of Torment' or 'Peak of Anxiety'	Here, you'll find the highest cliffs in any Scottish mountain range.
Sgurr na Banachdich	Perhaps from *banachdag*, 'a milkmaid'	This is a fine peak with three summits that are easy to bag.
Sgurr nan Gillean	'Peak of the Young Men'	This one is relatively isolated – 'a superb mountain' is one description – and the view from the top makes it all worthwhile.
Sgurr Mhic Choinnich	'MacKenzie's Peak'	Named after popular mountain guide, John MacKenzie,
Sgurr Dubh Mor	'Big Black Peak'	As well as being big and black, it's pretty impressive, providing a test even for experienced climbers.

Name	Translation	Comment
Am Basteir	Of obscure meaning	You must have a good head for heights for this one – and it's no place to have a slip. It has the Basteir Tooth which is regarded as the most difficult of all Munro tops and has been described by climbers as an 'intimidating fang of rock'.
Bla Bheinn (Blaven)	'Blue Hill' (Norse) or 'Warm Hill' (Gaelic)	The devotees describe this as a magnificent mountain, with one peak, Clach Glas – 'Grey Stone' – being nicknamed 'The Matterhorn of Skye'.
Sgurr nan Eag	'Peak of the Notches'	This one offers an easy climb, with many opportunities to relax and enjoy the views.
Sgurr a' Mhadaidh	'Peak of the Fox'	These four well-defined summits present some difficulties.

Mull

Name	Translation	Comment
Ben More	'The Big Hill'	It's the most westerly of Mull's main hills and it's Mull's highest mountain. There is a popular belief that it is the remains of a large volcano. Experts say there might have been lava flows centuries ago but it ain't no extinct volcano — just the only island Munro that's not in Skye.

Sport
and
Culture

The Burning of a Replica Viking Longship at Up-Helly-Aa

Up-Helly-Aa and Ba'

Shetlanders are proud of their Viking background and like to celebrate it in some style on the last Tuesday of January with a spectacular event called Up-Helly-Aa which is a lot younger than the Viking background.

Around 900 torch-bearing participants – men only – take to the streets of Lerwick behind a grand Viking longship. They are led through the darkened streets of the town by an annually appointed Guizer Jarl. His men, dressed as Vikings, brandish shields and silver axes and they set the longship alight by throwing their flaming torches into the galley while 'The Norseman's Home' is sung as a funeral dirge. There then follows a night of revelry as each of the forty-odd squads involved visit eleven local halls and put on wild and amusing sketches to entertain their hosts. Sleep is not on the agenda.

Up-Helly-Aa is not in itself all that ancient, dating only from Victorian times, but it replaced an older Christian tradition of burning tar barrels and rolling them through the streets. That was banned in 1874. It was seven years before Up-Helly-Aa appeared on the scene and it has been developed since.

In Orkney, they have another way of letting off steam and it is equally bizarre. They play the Orkney Ba' Game every Christmas and New Year's Day. According to the official rules – yes, apparently, there are some – the two sides are the Uppies and the Doonies or, more correctly, the 'Up-the-Gates' and the 'Doon-the-Gates' from the Old Norse *gata* meaning 'a path or road'. Originally, the side any individual played on was determined by whether he was born up or doon the gate but, nowadays, with recent housing developments, this tends to be based on family loyalties.

The game begins when the ball – the Men's Ba' which is handmade from leather and filled with cork – is thrown in the air at the Mercat Cross close to St Magnus Cathedral in

Kirkwall. It is pandemonium thereafter. The game is a mixture of football, rugby and disorder with as many as 200 men taking part and the ball is seen only occasionally. The Doonies have the harbour as their goal and the Uppies must get the ball to the top of the town to win. The game can last all day and dates from Norse times. The town takes on an appearance of siege during the Ba' Game, with shutters and barricades on all the shops and houses which might be on the Ba' route. Cars come near at their peril, while young children and elderly people are well advised to keep clear. But, according to the game's website, because of the camaraderie of the game, few players are hurt badly and, if the massive scrum collapses and someone is hurt or passes out, the game is stopped to allow the poor chap to be extricated.

Golf Courses

Scotland has more golf holes per head of population than almost anywhere else in the world. There are, in fact, around 550 golf courses and seventy golf ranges – and there are several opportunities to swing a club in some of the islands.

Arran

There are three eighteen-hole courses – at Brodick, Lamlash and Whiting Bay. They are all short courses – less than 4,700 yards. There is a unique twelve-hole links course at Shiskine near Blackwaterfoot and nine-hole courses at Corrie, Lochranza and Machrie.

Gigha

Golf was introduced to Gigha in the late 1800s when a team of local enthusiasts got together to design a course but as well as competing with each other, Gigha golfers have to compete with farming interests. Golf ceased around 1925 when the farming landowner decided that the land was best suited to agriculture and it was sixty years before the game returned to the island. This time it was another local committee which combined to lay out and create a new course but that course lasted only three years – once again it was the farmer who stymied the golfers. Club secretary John Bannatyne explains:

> The first time round, it was general agricultural use but the second time the farmer decided he could get more income from cows. He realised that golf and cows could not exist together. So, since 1989, we have had our third course – up until the millennium, we winter-grazed sheep on the course but the mess and tidying up in the spring was too much and it cost more than the income from the sheep. We now have a lease until 2008. The course is developing quite nicely and I would like to think it has a long-term future.

The Gigha Golf Club is affiliated to the Scottish Golf Union which means that, on the production of three score cards, members are issued with an official handicap and are eligible to take part in competitions anywhere.

Rothesay

The eighteen-hole Rothesay Golf Course was opened in 1892. The driving force, if you pardon the pun, behind the formation of the Rothesay Golf Club was John Windsor Stuart, factor to the Marquess of Bute, who pointed out the importance of 'having a golf course adjacent to a holiday resort like Rothesay'. The club professional, Jim Dougal, who co-wrote the club website, says the ground chosen for the nine-hole course was 'rough uncultured hill ground' but play on the course was soon in full swing. The green was opened by Mr A. Graham Murray, QC MP, who was captain of the club – and captain of the Royal and Ancient Golf Club. In 1908, the club moved to a new site which provided enough land for an eighteen-hole course and the Town Council invited James Braid, Harry Vardon, Arnaud Massy and Ben Sayers to play an exhibition match. James Braid and Harry Vardon were two of the triumvirate (the other being J. H. Taylor) who dominated British professional golf for twenty years before the First World War. Jim Douglas, who has been the club's pro for over fourteen years, says membership at Rothesay is now over 350. The club's first captain, Graham Murray, gifted a silver challenge cup – the Graham Murray Cleek – which has been up for annual competition between Rothesay and Millport (more about that later) for 111 years. Rothesay also has a thirteen-hole course at Port Bannatyne and a nine-hole course at Kingarth.

Cumbrae

From Rothesay Golf Club, you can look across the Firth of Clyde and see Cumbrae's Millport Golf Club. Each year, the two clubs compete for the aforementioned trophy. Millport has appointed a woman – Janet Frazer – as club secretary for the first time and she has 294 members under her care. She says the club started out as The Cumbrae Golf Club in 1888 and changed its name to Millport Golf Club to avoid confusion with the Comrie Golf Club in Perthshire. The eighteen-hole course is one of the longest established courses on the Firth of Clyde.

Barra

Established in 1992, the nine-hole course Isle of Barra Golf Club claims to be the UK's most westerly course. It has also resorted to using electrified fencing to keep the sheep off the course.

Harris

The Scarista Links, a nine-hole course at the Isle of Harris Golf Club, is certainly one with a difference. An article in the magazine *Golf International* listed what it calls the twelve golf courses in the world which are golf's 'glorious secrets' and the Harris course was chosen along with courses in the United States, South Africa, Australia, Thailand and Italy. The views at the Scarista course are stunning. The course was created in the 1930s, closed at the start of the Second World War and re-opened in 1985. Former European number one, Ronan Rafferty, opened the clubhouse while on a trip round the courses of the Western Isles. The members now come from all over the world. When Nick Faldo played there, he left an autographed fiver in the honesty box and club members now compete every year for the Faldo fiver.

Lewis

An eighteen-hole course at the Stornoway Golf Club, this one goes back a bit, having been founded in 1890. It is closely linked with the island's aviation past and began life on what is now the site of Stornoway Airport. The compensation it received from the Air Ministry when it took over the site paid for the move to its current home within the grounds of Lews Castle.

Benbecula

A nine-hole course at the Benbecula Golf Club, it was opened around 1985. Situated one mile from Benbecula Airport, it is set on grassland between the two Uists.

Islay

The eighteen-hole Machrie Golf Club, just outside Port Ellen, has huge dunes and rolling links and every hole is said to offer a challenge. In fact, this course has been rated Number 56 in *Golf World* 100, who describe it as 'a course designed by God, played by Man'.

Colonsay and Tiree

These islands have what are described as 'holiday' courses – a golfing friend has even described them as 'primitive' and says the best way to know where your ball has landed is by watching which of the grazing sheep scatter.

Mull

There is a nine-hole course at Tobermory which is described as having 'distinctive characteristics' and is more difficult than might be expected. There is also a nine-hole course – but with eighteen different tees – at Craignure.

Seil

This nine-hole course claims to be challenging with scenic views. How can it be challenging when there are no bunkers? Well, several holes are over water – and two of them are over the sea. Is that challenging enough?

Orkney

There are two eighteen-hole courses – the Orkney Golf Club and the Stromness Golf Club – and one nine-hole course at the Westray Golf Club. Orkney is a parkland course, opened with nine holes in 1902 after sterling work by members using horses and carts, picks and shovels. Nine more holes were added in 1923. Formed in 1890, Stromness has benefited from local and lottery investment and has a splendid club-house with bowling, tennis, sailing and football among the activities of what has become the Ness Sports and Social Club. Players at Westray are advised to look out for rabbit holes – is that what you could call a warrening?

Shetland

There are two eighteen-hole courses – one, the Shetland Golf Club, is five miles north of Lerwick and the other, Whalsay Golf Club, is five miles from the Symbister ferry terminal. The course at Whalsay is the most northerly eighteen-hole course in the UK. It was established in 1976 by a small group of fish-ermen. You need to make a short ferry crossing to get there.

Skye

There is one nine-hole course here, halfway between Broadford and Portree. It has nine greens but eighteen tees and there are spectacular views of the Cuillins and the island of Raasay.

South Uist

The nine-hole course at the Askernish Golf Club has been described by one golf website as 'without doubt one of Scotland's true hidden gems' and 'a nine-holer simply too good to miss'. You will find it five miles north west of Lochboisdale.

North Uist

A comparative newcomer, the nine-hole Sollas Golf Course on North Uist was built by local volunteers in 2001 and already has many visiting enthusiasts. The abundance of bird life is an added attraction – the eagles on this course can be of the winged variety.

Eriska

Here there is a golfing centre with a practice academy, a driving range and what is described as 'an emerging golf course' – the par is 22 for its 1,500 yards.

Easdale

You can actually play twelve islands here. Each hole is named after an island and, in putting order, they are: Tiree, Coll, Iona, Mull, Lismore, Easdale, Seil, Luing, Scarba, Colonsay, Jura and Islay.

Johnson and Boswell

In 1773, Samuel Johnson and James Boswell set off on what was to become their celebrated journey through the Highlands and on to the Hebrides. It was a journey which lasted eighty-three days and it seems that they were determined to write for posterity. The literary interplay between the two friends is still as fascinating as their comments on the islands, their hosts and the people they met. The language they used is a delight and they were undoubtedly the pioneers of sound bites.

The following are some of their comments on the Scottish islands:

Johnson on their dinner in Skye with Sir Alexander Macdonald:

> As we sat at Sir Alexander's table we were entertained, according to ancient usage of the North, with the melody of the bagpipe. Everything in those countries has its history. As the bagpiper was playing an elderly gentleman informed us that at some remote time the Macdonalds of Glengarry having been injured or offended by the inhabitants of Culloden where finding their enemies at worship they shut them up in the church which they set on fire; and this, said he, is the tune that the piper played while they were burning.

Johnson on Raasay:

> Raasay has little that can detain a traveller, except the laird and his family, but their power wants no auxiliaries. Such a feat of hospitality, amidst the winds and the waters, fills the imagination with a delightful, contrariety of images. Without is the rough ocean and the rocky land, the beating billows and the howling storm: within is plenty and elegance, beauty and gaiety, the song and the dance. In Raasay, if I could have found a Ulysses, I had fancied a Phaeacia.

Boswell on Skye:

> I must observe here that in Skye there seems to be much
> idleness; for men and boys follow you, as colts follow
> passengers upon a road. The usual figure of a Skye boy is a
> lown with bare legs and feet, a dirty kilt, ragged coat and
> waistcoat, a bare head and a stick in his hand, which, I
> suppose, is partly to help the lazy rogue to walk and partly to
> serve as a kind of defensive weapon.

Johnson on Skye:

> Skye is the greatest island or the greatest but one among the
> Hebrides. The gardens have apples and pears and cherries,
> strawberries, raspberries, currants and gooseberries, but all
> the fruit I have seen is small. They attempt to sow nothing
> but oats and barley: oats constitute the bread-corn of the
> place. They have seldom very hard frosts. Nor was it ever
> known that a lake was covered with ice strong enough to
> bear a skater. The animals here are not remarkably small,
> perhaps they recruit their breed from the mainland. The cows
> are sometimes without horns. The horned and unhorned
> cattle are not accidental variations but different species, they
> will however breed together.

Johnson again on Skye:

> Their food is not better than their lodging. They seldom taste
> the flesh of land animals for here there are no markets.
> What each man eats is from his own flock. The great effect
> of money is to break property into small parts. In towns, he
> that has a shilling may have a piece of meat; but where there
> is no commerce no man can eat mutton but by killing a
> sheep. Tea is always drunk at the usual times, but in the
> morning the table is polluted with a plate of slices of strong
> cheese. Strong liquors they seem to love; every man, perhaps
> woman, begins the day with a dram and the punch is made
> both at dinner and supper.

Johnson on Coll and Tiree:

> *There are sometimes beggars who wander from island to island. We had, in our passage to Mull, the company of a woman and her child who had exhausted the charity of Coll. The arrival of a beggar on an island is accounted a sinistrous event. Everybody considers that he shall have less for what he gives away. Their alms, I believe, are generally oatmeal. Near to Col is an island called Tireye, eminent for its fertility. Though it has half the extent of Rum it is so well peopled that there have appeared, not long ago, nine hundred and fourteen at a funeral. In Skye what is wanted can only be bought, as the arrival of some wandering peddler may afford an opportunity; but in Col there is a standing shop, and in Mull there are two. A shop in the islands, as in other places of little frequentation, is a repository of everything requisite for common use.*

Johnson on Ulva, Mull:

> *We were introduced to Mr Macquarry, the head of a small clan, whose ancestors have reigned in Ulva beyond memory but who has reduced himself by his negligence and folly to the necessity of selling this venerable patrimony.*

Boswell on Ulva:

> *Macquarry's house was mean; but we were agreeably surprised with the appearance of the master, whom we found to be intelligent, polite and much a man of the world. Though his clan is not numerous, he is a very ancient chief, and has a burial place at Icolmkill. He told us his family had possessed Ulva for nine hundred years but I was distressed to hear that it was soon to be sold for the payment of his debts.*

Around the time of the Johnson and Boswell visit, young Lachlan Macquarry, born on Ulva, was about twelve and he was to go on to earn himself the title of 'Father of Australia', instituting liberal reforms in the country while serving as

Governor of New South Wales. But this did not bring him popularity and he lost the job. His mausoleum is on Mull. And fifteen years after the visit of the literary duo, Neil Livingstone, father of David Livingstone, was born on Ulva. The failure of the potato crop in the early 1790s led to most of the 600 inhabitants of Ulva leaving Scotland for America or Canada. In 1865, eight years before his death, David Livingstone paid a nostalgic visit to Ulva, which he regarded as his ancestral home.

Johnson on Iona:

> *Iona has long enjoyed, without any very credible attestation, the honour of being reputed as the cemetery of the Scottish kings. It is not unlikely, that, when the opinion of local sanctity was prevalent, the chieftains of the isles, and perhaps for of the Norwegian or Irish princes were reposited in this venerable enclosure. But by whom the subterranean vaults are peopled is now utterly unknown. The graves are very numerous, and some of them undoubtedly contain the remains of men, who did not expect to be soon forgotten.*

He described it as 'this awful ground'.

Johnson on leaving the Hebrides:

> *Of these islands it must be confessed that they have not many allurements but to the mere lover of naked nature. The inhabitants are thin, provisions are scarce and desolation and penury give little pleasure.*

Film Locations

Given the beauty, solitude and romantic atmosphere of the Scottish islands, it is surprising that the film-makers have not made more use of them. Perhaps it is due to the comparative inaccessibility and remoteness which makes it expensive to transport film crews and all that they bring with them. Skye has been the popular choice for film-makers, followed by Mull.

Skye

Bonnie Prince Charlie (Anthony Kimmins, 1948)
An eminently forgettable film that has David Niven in the starring role as the Young Pretender. A lot of the exterior stuff was filmed on Skye but critics say it was let down by appalling studio sets. Margaret Leighton, Jack Hawkins, Finlay Currie and John Laurie also star.

Breaking the Waves (Lars von Trier, 1996)
This has to be one of the best films ever made on the islands – it won the Grand Jury Prize at the Cannes Film Festival in 1996. The film was a joint effort between Denmark, Sweden, France and the Netherlands, featuring a little-known cast. A young woman in a remote part of Scotland humiliates herself in the hope of saving the life of her husband who has been paralysed in an oil rig accident.

The Brothers (David Macdonald, 1947)
An orphan girl brings all sorts of problems to an island fishing family in a tale of superstition, sexual jealousy and, eventually, tragedy. Patricia Roc and Maxwell Reed get the lead parts but it is Duncan Macrae who steals the film.

Captain Jack (Robert Young, 1998)

This kids' tale, about a sailor on an anniversary trip to the Arctic on an unseaworthy vessel with an amateur crew, starts out in Skye. Bob Hoskins and Gemma Jones head the cast.

Highlander (Russell Mulcahy, 1986)

Sean Connery stars, along with Christopher Lambert, in what has been described as a 'muddled fantasy' about a sixteenth-century Scotsman who apparently dies in battle but finds he is immortal. The makers of the three sequels and a TV series deserted Skye, choosing foreign locations instead.

Monty Python and the Holy Grail (Terry Gilliam and Terry Jones, 1975)

They searched for the Holy Grail everywhere with most of the scenes shot in Scotland and some in Skye.

The Wicker Man (Robin Hardy, 1973)

This has become a cult movie. This is a chilling story about a policeman (played by Edward Woodward) who flies to a remote Scottish island to investigate the death of a child and comes to a fiery end. It was filmed mainly in south-west Scotland but the opening island scenes were of Skye.

Mull

Entrapment (Jon Amiel, 1999)

Sean Connery finds himself at Duart Castle along with Catherine Zeta-Jones in a tale about a female insurance investigator who sets a trap for the world's greatest thief by asking him to steal a Chinese mask worth millions. Critics say it is a thriller-cum-comedy which gets by thanks to its 'lustrous settings'. Cheers Mull.

Eye of the Needle (Richard Marquand, 1981)

This is a spy story about a German agent who murders his landlady but is found out by a girl. Donald Sutherland and Kate Nelligan are the stars.

I Know Where I'm Going (Michael Powell and Emeric Pressburger, 1945)

This is about a determined girl (Wendy Hiller) travelling to the Hebrides to marry a wealthy old man but she is stranded on Mull and marries a young naval officer instead. It was shot on Colonsay as well as Mull and Duart Castle is featured. It stars Roger Livesay and John Laurie and Finlay Currie are in this one also.

Madame Sin (David Greene, 1972)

In this TV movie, Bette Davis made a rare appearance on Mull in this tale about a CIA agent being used as a pawn in an insane woman's plan to steal a Polaris submarine. Robert Wagner, Catherine Schell and Denholm Elliott also star.

When Eight Bells Toll (Etienne Périer, 1971)

Dervaig on Mull was one of the locations for this Alistair MacLean tale about the pirating of gold bullion ships off the Scottish coast, with Anthony Hopkins in the lead. He stayed at the Old Ferry House, which is where cattlemen stayed in days of yore. Then, of course, film-making was not what they had in mind – they had other reasons for lingering and that is why the house became known as a house of ill repute. Some of the scenes were shot on Staffa.

Foula

The Edge of the World (Michael Powell, 1937)

This film was inspired by the evacuation in 1930 of the remote island of St Kilda, 100 miles west of the Scottish mainland.

The writer/director, Michael Powell, was refused permission to film on St Kilda so he went instead to Foula, a reasonable lookalike. In *Halliwell's Film Guide* it is described as 'life, love and death on Foula, a vigorous location drama, sometimes naïve, sometimes exhilarating'. The story centres on two families, headed by John Laurie and Finlay Currie.

Seil Island

Ring of Bright Water (Jack Couffer, 1969)

Seil Island near Oban was the setting for this delightful story about a man who buys a pet otter and moves to a remote cottage in Scotland. Bill Travers and his wife Virginia McKenna star.

Harris

2001: A Space Odyssey (Stanley Kubrick, 1968)

This is pushing it a bit but I'm that kind of guy – aerial shots of the east coast of Harris were used to represent the planet Jupiter in this major sci-fi film.

Barra

Whisky Galore (Alexander Mackendrick, 1949)

In the United States, they called it *Tight Little Island*. The film did not disappoint with its version of the Compton Mackenzie novel about the *SS Politician* which ran aground in 1941 with 50,000 cases of whisky on board. It was taking the whisky to the United States, hoping to avoid the German U-boats in the Atlantic but it could not avoid the rocks off Eriskay. The islanders made sure the crew was safe before they pounced on the whisky. Then HM Customs and Excise spoiled it all by appearing on the scene.

In 1989, a company was formed to salvage any whisky remaining in the wreck but they could find only a few bottles.

The islanders had clearly done their job well. Although all this happened off Eriskay, after careful deliberation and a few visits to other islands, the film-makers chose Barra for what was the first Ealing comedy to be made entirely on location. Some scenes were also filmed on Vatersay, now linked to Barra by a causeway. Basil Radford, Gordon Jackson and Duncan Macrae were among the stars. A sequel, *Rockets Galore*, described by one critic as 'amiable but disappointing', was also shot on Barra.

Mysteries, Tragedies and Tall Stories

The Vanishing Lighthouse Keepers

The disappearance of three lighthouse keepers on the Flannan Islands was one of the mysteries of the twentieth century. You can read all about it in the Lighthouses chapter of this book but, in summary, in December 1900, Flannan's three lighthouse keepers simply vanished. The assumption was that they were the victims of a freak wave but the mystery became a fearful bedtime story for Victorian children. It also became the subject of a poem by Wilfred Gibson and a modern opera by Peter Maxwell Davies. The lighthouse became automatic in 1971 but, for those seventy-one manned years, lighthouse keepers doing their stint there must have been more than a little nervous. The Flannan Islands are part of a chain of islands twenty miles west of Lewis. They are known as the Seven Hunters because of their reputation for claiming ships.

The Brownie of Cara

The Brownie of Cara is said to be the ghost of a Macdonald murdered by a Campbell – perish the thought! Tradition says he lives in an attic in Cara House and that the laird and minister have always raised their hats to him when they step ashore at Cara – and so should everybody else. There is one story about two men who went to fetch a cask of wine from the cellar at Cara House. They had a bit of banter about the brownie and he seemed to retaliate because, surprisingly, they found they could not move the cask. They offered a sincere apology for their jocular approach to the brownie – and the barrel suddenly ran up the plank leading from the cellar by itself, bounced and rolled across the ground to the sea, before coming to a stop beside the men's boat. Chances are they had been at the wine beforehand.

Julian, Gregorian or Both?

Foula, one of the remote islands of Shetland, is the island of two Christmases. It stuck to the Roman Julian calendar when Scotland and most of Europe went over to the Gregorian calendar in 1600 and, even after the rest of Britain adopted the Gregorian in 1752, the Foula islanders stuck to their Julian guns and continue to do so. Islanders and some incomers celebrate Christmas on 6 January and New Year's Day is 13 January. Others follow the usual dates – but some can see the attraction of opting for both.

Reports of her Death Have Been Greatly Exaggerated

From Duart Castle in Mull you can see Lady's Rock and this was some lady. Long ago, a MacLean chieftain married the Earl of Argyll's sister. The marriage was a failure – he claimed his wife had twice tried to poison him – so, in 1523, he tied her up and marooned her on the rock. The next morning, seeing from the castle that she had been washed away by the tide, he sadly reported her death to her brother. The Earl wanted her to be buried in Inveraray and, in due course, MacLean and his retinue appeared with a sealed coffin. He was shown into the dining hall where he was astonished and somewhat dismayed to see his wife sitting at the top table next to her brother. It seems that she had been rescued by a passing fisherman. MacLean somehow got through the meal and was allowed to leave. But his days were numbered – some time later he was discovered murdered in his bed in Edinburgh.

You Started It – No, We Didn't, You Did

There have been some nasty incidents on Eigg. St Donan set up a large monastery there in 617 but was murdered together with fifty-two of his monks. Then, in 1577, some MacLeods from Skye were sent home castrated after being caught raping MacDonald girls on Eigg. The MacLeods were more than a little upset and returned to get their own back, if you see what I mean. Close on 400 MacDonalds hid in a cave and were missed by the MacLeod landing party who only found one old woman and spared her life. But, as they were putting out to sea, they saw a scout who had been sent from the cave to see if the coast was clear. The MacLeods rushed back and tried to smoke the MacDonalds out by lighting a brushwood fire in the entrance. Every MacDonald is said to have suffocated in the smoke. The cave is still known as Massacre Cave. Sir Walter Scott is said to have found bones here in 1814 and taken a souvenir away with him. Several people claim to have seen ghosts here.

In 1579, on Skye the MacLeods were attending a service at Trumpan Church when they were attacked by – yes, you've guessed it – the MacDonalds of South Uist who set fire to the church and massacred the congregation. One girl escaped, severing her breast as she squeezed through a narrow window, and she raised the alarum. As the MacDonalds, with MacLeod blood on their hands, returned to their boats the MacLeods were waiting . . . another massacre.

The last battle to be fought in Scotland using just swords and bows and arrows was the Battle of Carinish in North Uist in 1601 between the MacDonalds of Uist and the MacLeods of Harris. The cause of the battle appears to have been the insulting behaviour of one of the MacDonalds who divorced his MacLeod wife and sent her home. You could say that, in those days, a MacDonald marrying a MacLeod was just asking for trouble and did he get it – the MacLeods descended on Carinish in a frenzy and, in the furious battle that ensued, all but two of them were killed. The site of the battle is known as *Feith-na-Fala*, the Field of Blood.

Not Horsing Around

Eilean Choraidh, also known as Horse Island, was reckoned to look like the German battleship *Tirpitz* and was used by British Mosquito bombers for target practice during the Second World War. The 1931 census had recorded a population of one male on the island but we don't know if he was still there when the bombers attacked – it would have been quite a shock for him if he had repaired to Horse Island to get away from it all.

Nicolson's Leap

On South Uist there is Nicolson's Leap. The story goes that a member of the Nicolson Clan was found in bed with the wife of the Clan Ranald chief – certainly not something you undertook if you wanted to prolong your life. As he escaped, he snatched the chief's baby son as a hostage and, while fleeing from the outraged clansmen, he leapt a 15-metre chasm on to a rock. From there, he tried to bargain with his pursuers but they would have none of it – so the errant Nicolson jumped to his death in the sea, taking the boy with him.

Love Flies out the Window

Fuday on the island of Barra is supposed to have been the last retreat for a bunch of Norsemen who were on King Haakon's losing side at the Battle of Largs in 1263. The battle was not meant to have taken place – the longships of King Haakon and his Vikings were blown ashore by a gale and, as they struggled through the surf, the Scots bade them welcome with a battle. Both sides claimed a victory but the small band of Vikings retreated north to Fuday and abandoned their territorial claims to the Western Isles three years later. Fuday is a name possibly derived from the Norse *utey* which means an outside isle. It should have been a safe haven for the weary Vikings but, according to that good old source, tradition, an illegitimate son of MacNeil of Barra wished to ingratiate himself with his family so he sought and caught the attention of one of the Norse maidens on Fuday. She fell in love with him and, in their thirteenth-century pillow talk, she gave him detailed information about the Norse defences. That's when love flew out the window and the bold boy then led a raid on the island and wiped out the entire population. Fuday actually had a population of seven in 1861 but is has long since been deserted – apart from the Norse graves.

A Trying Time

Along the western shores of Arran is a series of natural caves in the sandstone rock. It was in one of these caves, known as the King's Caves, that Robert the Bruce found refuge and supposedly had his famed encounter with the persistent spider which could claim to have changed the course of Scottish history.

MacLeod Memorabilia

St Clement's Church on Harris is described as a gloomy, atmospheric church, dating from the 1520s. The church houses many monuments to the MacLeod Clan from Dunvagan and Harris – and more. There are many sculpted reliefs depicting a number of scenes, some of them religious and some blatantly sexual, with pagan overtones and depicting genitalia. Built in the sixteenth century, it stands on the foundations of a much earlier building, probably from the thirteenth century, when the church was first dedicated.

Cuithach's Heilan' Hame

Dun Borranish, Uig, Lewis, is a ruined dun or stone-built hill fort that is believed to be the place that the giant Cuithach called home. Like many of his kind, he was in the business of laying waste to the surrounding area by indulging in cattle rustling and bumping off the locals. Eventually the bodyguards of the local chief, known as the Fians, trapped and killed him. The story goes that the giant's grave is some distance away from his home at the ruined dun.

A Fishy Tail

At Nunton on Benbecula, there is a ruined chapel which belonged to a nunnery whose nuns were brutally massacred when the building was destroyed during the Reformation. And there's more – rumour has it that a mermaid is buried in the

Nunton sands. In 1830, some women who were on the fore-shore gathering seaweed spotted a mermaid in the shallow waters not far out to sea. Although they tried to catch her, she was too quick and too smart for them. A son of one of the women began to throw pebbles at her. One seemed to strike her and she dropped from view into the water. A few days later, a wee body, that was said to have its top half in the form of a young child and the lower part resembling a salmon but without scales, was washed ashore. She was wrapped in a shawl, placed in a specially made small coffin and buried above the highest tide mark. Aye, right.

Islanders Do it More Fruitfully

Official figures released in December 2004 showed that it was the Scottish island communities who recorded Scotland's highest birth rates in 2003. In Shetland, 251 babies were born, giving a general fertility rate (GFR) of 61.4 births per 1,000 women of child-bearing age. This compares with a GFR of 57.3 per 1,000 in the Western Isles, where 255 infants were born. According to *The Scotsman* newspaper, the Western Isles have made it their mission to better Shetland's higher rate in the coming months. A spokesman for the Western Isles Health Board said, 'A few more dark evenings and a hard winter should mean we will beat Shetland next year.'

Unusual Eating Habits

You can be well fed in the islands, especially on Lewis and Skye.

Bonaventure, a restaurant in a former RAF barracks perched on the top of a 600-ft high cliff in Lewis, has become the first restaurant in the Western Isles to make its way into the prestigious *Michelin Guide*. The restaurant, which serves up a delightful mix of French and Scottish cuisine, has been awarded one knife and fork status in the 2004 guide, the first step towards a full Michelin star. Skye's famous Three Chimneys Restaurant – named in other guides as among the thirty best restaurants in the world – received two knives and forks. So there is undoubtedly some superb cuisine in the islands. However, although, in many of the islands, you can buy books of local recipes, they are not actually that local – there are not many typical island dishes apart from those which contain local fare such as venison and trout.

Kale along with porridge have been the staple diet of most Scots for centuries and, if you really need to warm up, you should try the Shetland winter dish of 'kail and knockit corn' which is kale and porridge oats.

The making of cheese on the Scottish islands has long been practised as a way of conserving the rich plentiful milk of the spring and early summer. The islands of Bute, Arran, Islay, Orkney and Mull all produce some superb cheeses that bring something tasty to the cheese board. Arran has a caboc, which is rolled in oatmeal and is based on a rediscovered Highland recipe, and Gigha produces an excellent goat's cheese.

Arran does not stop at cheese – the island produces handmade chocolates, oatcakes, smoked fish, preserves, chutneys, ice cream and marmalades.

In *Recipes from the Orkney Islands*, for example, the introduction states that priority has been given to what is considered to be original recipes with a distinctive Orkney flavour, using local produce such as meat, seafood, cheese, grain, sweetmeats, whisky and so on. Orkney ice cream is very popular on the mainland. It's the same with many of the other island recipe books that we sampled – good local produce, dishes with a variation, dishes that are just slightly different and given an island name, but there are not many island recipes that have travelled. However, that does not mean to say there are no unusual eating habits on some of the islands. They are distinctive, to be sure, but you will not find them in any recipe book or on any restaurant menu. You will not be terribly anxious to bring them to your own table.

Top of the list must be an annual snack enjoyed by the young men of a place called Nis on Lewis. Every August, for at least 400 years, young men from the island have set off from Port Nis to harvest the young gannets, known as gugas, that nest in their thousands on a remote, uninhabited – by humans – rock called Sula Sgeir, forty-one miles due north. They will spend a fortnight on Sula and, during that time, will slaughter 2,000 young gannets. The birds are killed with a stick, decapitated, singed in a fire, pickled in salt and sold as a delicacy for more than £15 a pair. Hundreds of people eagerly wait the return of the men with their haul. Not surprisingly, this annual sortie has its opponents. It is not popular with the Royal Society for the Protection of Birds but, nonetheless, it does give its blessing, as does Scottish Natural Heritage, and the Scottish Executive provides a special cull licence.

It seems that boiled gannet and potato is a popular Lewis delicacy. There is never any shortage of guga hunt volunteers for the annual cull and feast of what has been described as oily flesh which is definitely an acquired taste.

Over on the east coast, the Bass Rock has the largest colony of gannets on the east coast of Britain and holds about 10% of the world population of North Atlantic gannets. Sir Hew Dalrymple, Lord President of the Court of Session and 1st Baron of North Berwick, bought the rock from the Crown in one of the last acts of the old Scottish parliament, before its dissolution in 1707. He rented the rock to a tenant who had the right to graze sheep on the rock's seven acres of grass – and he was also allowed to hunt the gannets in season. The gannets – they were marketed in those days as solan geese – were sold in Edinburgh for 20 old pence each to butchers based in the High Street at Fleshers Close. In 1870, twenty-five sheep were still being grazed on the island and Bass mutton was a famous and favourite eighteenth-century Edinburgh delicacy but the island's principal produce for the table was young gannets. According to www.north-berwick.co.uk/bass, the young gannet flesh was described as 'excellent' if skinned and it was cooked like beefsteak.

But please do not turn your nose up at the thought of gannet on a plate. Gannet eggs, after all, had royal approval. Gannet's eggs often graced Queen Victoria's breakfast table. The killing, or 'harrying' as it was called, of the young birds on the Bass Rock was carried out by men with ropes round their bodies, the ends of which were held by others on the top. They descended the cliff, stepping from nest to nest, knocking the young birds on the head and throwing them into the sea where others in boats were waiting to pick them up and off they went to the restaurants. It was a different technique from that used by the guga hunters of Lewis and, while the Bass cull of gannets/gugas/solan geese has long since gone, the practice still has official approval on Lewis.

Then there are the deer on the island of Rum. Sometimes it is spelled Rhum but you should get the h out of it – Rum it is. Some say the 'h' was introduced in Victorian times because of sensitivities about strong drink but, if you pronounce it correctly, it sounds the same as room. But back to the Rum deer – they supplement their normally vegetarian diet by devouring live seabird chicks. Scientists believe that the normally docile beasts eat the baby birds to make up for deficiencies in their diet – or are maybe using them as a form of medicine. The main bird on the deer menu is the Manx shearwater and the deer settle for the heads only.

On North Ronaldsay, Orkney's most northerly island, the sheep are unique. Tough and goat-like, they don't stick to a diet of grass. They mostly eat seaweed (except when lambing) which gives their flesh a dark tone – a 'delicious dark mutton' as one visitor described it – and a rich, gamey taste. Top London restaurants are among the customers. And their thick wool is highly prized. The sheep are owned by the community and the flock is maintained at around 4,000 head, with each family having an agreed allocation according to an elected committee – the Sheep Court. An offshore oil spill would be a disaster for the seaweed supply so the wily islanders now have a small flock of their sheep kept in England as a safeguard.

Residents on the island of Easedale, south of Oban, used to use seaweed as an additional source of nourishment, the most favoured variety being Carrageen or Iceland Moss. This, when boiled, became a gelatinous mess, rich in protein and easily swallowed. It was said to be particularly useful for feeding infants and the sick and elderly.

The North Ronaldsay sheep are not the only ones with unusual diets – sheep on the island of Foula have been spotted eating live tern and skua.

Work

The Isle of Jura Distillery

Distilleries

The term whisky comes from the Gaelic *uisge beatha* or *usque-baugh*, meaning water of life. It has been distilled in Scotland for hundreds of years. There is some evidence to show that the art of distilling could have been brought to the country by Christian missionary monks.

According to information supplied by the Scotch Whisky Association, the earliest historical reference to whisky comes much later. J Marshall Robb, in his book *Scotch Whisky: A Guide*, says: 'The oldest reference to whisky occurs in the Scottish Exchequer Rolls for 1494 when there was an entry of "eight bols of malt to Friar John Cor wherewith to make aqua-vitae". A boll was an old Scottish measure of not more than six bushels and six bushels are equivalent to 152.4 kilograms, which would be enough barley to make around 1,500 bottles.

There are two kinds of Scotch whisky – malt whisky, which is made using what is called the pot still process, and grain whisky, which is made by the patent still process. Malt whisky is made from malted barley only while grain whisky is made from malted barley together with unmalted barley and other cereals.

I would suggest that malt whisky is for the purist. I have heard it described as a slippers-by-the-fire drink and the only thing you put into malt is more malt although a wee drop of water – a teardrop – will undoubtedly enhance the flavour.

If two whiskies are blended together, the result is what they call, believe it or not, a blend. You can add what you like to a blend but my preference is a fair amount of ice. A blend will consist of anything from fifteen to fifty different whiskies, combined in the proportions of a formula that is the secret of the blending company concerned.

The Scotch Whisky Association divides the malt whiskies into four groups according to the geographical location of the distilleries in which they are made. They are: Lowland malt whiskies, made south of an imaginary line drawn from Dundee in the east, through Perth and on to Greenock in the west; Highland malt whiskies, made north of that line; Speyside malt whiskies, from the valley of the River Spey (although these whiskies come from within the area designated as Highland malt whiskies, the concentration of distilleries and the specific climatic conditions produce a whisky of identifiable character and they, therefore, require a separate classification); and Islay malt whiskies. Campbeltown is sometimes listed as a fifth whisky region – it once had about thirty distilleries but now there are only two.

Each group has its own clearly defined characteristics, ranging from the lighter Lowland malt whiskies to those distilled on Islay which are generally regarded as the heaviest malt whiskies. Geographically, the boundaries are blurred because some of them were based on areas covered by regulatory authorities for licences and duties. So forget the geography, take a deep breath, charge your glass and read on for this tour of island distilleries. By the way, The Scotch Malt Whisky Society say that the straight-sided, cut-crystal tumbler, usually referred to as a whisky glass, is fine for its intended purpose but it's unsuited to the subtlety of malt whisky, for which a sherry copita or small brandy glass is much more appropriate.

Islay

Islay (pronounced 'eye-luh') is only twenty-five miles long but it is home to nine distilleries – at one time that figure was over twenty-five. The whiskies from this area have more than a hint of saltiness due to the fact that Islay is frequently lashed by Atlantic storms. Sea spray blows across the island, impregnating the peat used in the malting of the barley and finding its way into the warehouses where casks of Scotch whiskies are maturing ('Shhh! Whisky sleeping' is a sign you will see in some whisky warehouses), thus affecting the taste and the aroma. The result is that some of the Islay whiskies are pungent and powerful, with a distinctive whiff of sea air in them.

Other distilleries, which are in a more sheltered location and use less peat during malting, will have a gentler but still clearly identifiable character.

The Islay distilleries:

Ardbeg, near Port Ellen

Believed to have first been operational in 1794, it was founded by Alexander Stewart but he went out of business the same year. It was revived in 1815 by John MacDougall and, in 1979, became part of Hiram Walker who later merged with Allied Domecq (who have Allied Distillers). It was closed down – mothballed is the term – from 1981 until 1989 and there was only intermittent production between 1990 and 1996. Then Glenmorangie took it over in 1997 and successfully revived the business. In 2004, Glenmorangie put itself up for sale and after considerable international interest it was bought for £300 million by Louis Vuitton Moet Hennessy, the French luxury goods group who promise a bright future for Ardbeg.

Bowmore

Founded in 1779, it has four stills and an excellent visitor centre. It is one of the few malt whisky distilleries to produce its own floor-malted barley which is hand turned by the maltman using traditional malt shovels. The whisky is aged in Spanish and American oak casks in damp cellars below sea level. It is owned by Morrison Bowmore which is part of the Japanese conglomerate, Suntory.

Bruichladdich

Whisky it might be but to say its name you begin with 'Brew' and each 'ch' thereafter is pronounced as in loch – try saying that after a couple of nips. The distillery sits on some of the oldest rocks in Scotland – amphibolite gneiss which was formed about 1800 million years ago. It was built in 1881 by three brothers using money left in trust by their father (who had made his money with the Yoker distillery in Glasgow). It was closed down in 1927 and the warehouses were badly damaged during the Clydebank blitz in 1941. In the eyes of its then American owners, Jim Beam Brands, it became a mill-stone and was closed down in 1994 and it fell into disrepair. It was bought from the American owners by four enthusiasts in December 2002 and it is now alive and well again. They have installed webcams so that people from around the world can watch the whisky being made. The distillery hit the head-lines when the Pentagon admitted it was using the webcams to spy on the distillery because they thought it was a plant for the manufacture of weapons of mass destruction – as opposed to mass delectation! It is currently owned by Bruichladdich Distillery Company Ltd.

Bunnahabhain

This one's pronounced 'boon-a-hab-in' – another delightful tongue-twister. Situated near Port Askaig, it was founded in 1880. Now owed by Burn Stewart Distillers, the distillery is set around a courtyard in a style not unlike that of a chateau in Bordeaux.

Caol Ila

Pronounced 'cool eela', this distillery takes its name from the Gaelic for the Sound of Islay, the strait that separates Islay from Jura. Also near Port Askaig, it has a delightful outlook. It was built in 1846 by Hector Henderson. It was silent – i.e. not operational – from 1941 until 1945 because of wartime restrictions on the supply of barley to distillers. Rebuilt and extended in 1972, it is now owned by Diageo.

Lagavulin

The 'vu' is pronounced 'voo'. There are two distilleries on this site. The earlier one was founded in 1816 by John Johnston – it was the first legal distillery on Islay which, as early as 1742, had around ten illicit stills. The second came a year later and was built by Archibald Campbell. It continued to operate until at least 1833, trading under the name of Ardmore. It was also a casualty of wartime restrictions. After Johnston's death in 1836, the two were amalgamated when the Glasgow-based Islay malt merchant Alexander Graham, to whom Johnston had been in debt, acquired Lagavulin for the princely sum of £1,103 9s 8d. The ruins of Dunyveg Castle, a stronghold of the MacDonalds, are at the distillery entrance. A subsequent owner, Peter Mackie, became famous throughout the whisky world as the creator of the famous blend, White Horse. This one is also owned by Diageo.

Laphroaig

Pronounced 'laugh-ro-aig', this distillery is also near Port Ellen. It was founded in 1815 – and, curiously, the founder died in 1847 after falling into a vat of partially made whisky. Enlarged in 1923, its malt whisky was the first to be officially supplied to a member of the royal family – Prince Charles – and it now proudly bears the words 'By Appointment' on its label. It also boasts another distinction – it was the only whisky permitted to be sold in the United States during Prohibition. Apparently, this was because it was believed to have medicinal qualities – an excuse I often use. The site is where the Ardenistle Distillery operated from 1837 until 1848. Laphroaig is now owned by Allied Distillers.

Jura

Jura is known as 'Stag Island', a reference to its red deer population. It's a lonely lovely island and is the place George Orwell repaired to in isolation to warn us all about 1984. The island's first official distillery was built at Craighouse in 1810 but there is evidence that illicit distilling had been taking place from as far back as 1502. In its initial years, the distillery was let out to many people but, in the early 1900s, there was a dispute which led to the owners shutting it down and dismantling and selling the machinery. The roofs were removed to avoid paying rates and the distillery became a ruin. From 1960 to 1963, it was rebuilt by Scottish & Newcastle Breweries and was subsequently taken over by Invergordon Distillers in 1985. In 1995, it was bought by Whyte and Mackay, part of American Brands.

Arran

Arran Distillery is also known as Lagg. It was opened in 1995 and describes itself as the first legal distillery on Arran for nearly 200 years. Its visitor centre was opened by the Queen in 1997 and is well worth a visit. Early in the nineteenth century there were more than fifty whisky stills on Arran, most of them illegal and carefully hidden from the eyes of the taxman. It is privately owned by the Isle of Arran Distillers (created by Andrew Currie with his father) and its products are the Arran malt and the Lochranza blend plus Holy Isle Cream Liqueur – all of which are sold in nearly thirty countries.

Mull

Tobermory Distillery is also known as Ledaig. Established by John Sinclair in 1798, it was silent between 1930 and 1972. It re-opened in 1972 and was bought from the receiver in 1978 by a Yorkshire company who revived it and then sold it to its current owners, Burn Stewart, in 1993.

Skye

The Talisker Distillery was founded at Carbost in 1830 by Hugh and Kenneth MacAskill who hailed from the island of Eigg. The setting-up of this distillery happened much to the disgust of a local minister who had a zeal for total abstinence. He described its establishment at Carbost as 'one of the greatest curses that, in the ordinary course of Providence, could befall it or any other place'. It was closed from 1941 to 1945 as a result of wartime difficulties, including severe restrictions on the supply of barley to distillers. After a fire in the stillhouse in 1960, it was rebuilt and re-opened in 1962. It is now owned by Diageo. Robert Louis Stevenson described the strong, peaty Talisker as the 'king o' drinks'.

Orkney

Highland Park Distillery, Kirkwall

This one was founded in 1795 and is Scotland's most northerly distillery – just beating the distillery at Scapa for this distinction. It was closed during the Second World War, when the army used it as a food store and the huge vats served as communal baths – which, no doubt, later gave the whisky extra body. It is owned by Edrington Distillers.

Scapa

Opened in 1885, it overlooks Scapa Flow. It was rebuilt in 1959 and has been mothballed since 1994. However, it is undergoing an extensive refurbishment and will be re-opened. It is owned by Allied Distillers.

Despite claims that vodka is now Scotland's spirit of choice, the whisky business is booming and new distilleries are in the pipeline.

Shetland

Blackwood Distillers have plans to build a distillery on the site of an abandoned First World War airfield, ten miles north of Lerwick. Shetland Enterprise has approved funding for the project and there is also backing from the Bank of Scotland and private investors. It is hoped that the first whisky will roll out in late 2007 or early 2008, and when that happens, it will displace Highland Park as Scotland's most northerly distillery.

Barra

Andrew Currie, who, along with his father, founded the Isle of Arran Distillery, has plans for the first distillery (well, the first legal one) on Barra. He has identified the site, set up a company, appointed architects and arranged the finance with a spring 2005 target in mind for building to start. The name of the company is Uisge Beatha nan Eilean (The Island Whisky Company) and it will distil a tiny 25,000 litres a years, making it one-twentieth the size of Scotland's smallest distillery, Edradour, near Pitlochry. Mr Currie plans a visitor centre and will give the Barra community an opportunity to buy up to 10% of the shares of the company.

Newspapers

As well as the Scottish and UK national papers – whose arrival times often depend on the weather – many of the islands have their own newspapers. Some are actually in the form of newsletters that are published weekly or fortnightly – or every so often – but they still serve their purpose.

Island journalism is not a douce little retreat for retired hacks or hopeful beginners. In some cases, the competition can be as hot and as cut-throat as anywhere on the mainland and the quality of some of the newspapers is as high as you will find anywhere.

Orkney

Is a particularly hot spot for journalism. It's not often that you see a major launch of a newspaper on the islands to take on an established publication but that is what has happened on Orkney. *Orkney Today* was launched in October 2003 to take on the long-established paper *The Orcadian*. Its success proved that Orcadians like to read two local newspapers – *Orkney Today* has built up a circulation of 5,722 and the circulation of *The Orcadian* has gone up slightly to 11,323.

Shetland

The competition is even hotter here. *The Shetland Times*, published in Lerwick, with a circulation of more than 11,000, has been around some time, having been founded in 1872. The company that owns it has been in the same family for four generations and it also publishes books of local interest, with almost sixty titles on its list. It had it all to itself until along came an upstart in 1996 in the shape of Jonathan Mills. He had once worked with the owner of *The Shetland Times* but they went their separate ways and both set up web sites. Wills claimed he had launched *The Shetland News* as Britain's first daily internet paper and five months later *The Shetland Times* claimed it was the first Scottish weekly newspaper to go on-line. The two squabbled over who could do what and the dispute went as far as the Court of Session in Edinburgh. Judgement was passed down, with *The Shetland News* apparently the happier of the two with the outcome. It had taken its name from a weekly newspaper which had been published in Shetland between 1885 and 1963. In 1999 *The Shetland News* web site, which used to attract 20,000 to 30,000 readers daily, was abandoned because of lack of funds but, in March 2003, the concept and the name was bought by a German journalist, Hans Marter, and a former *Shetland Times* journalist, Pete Bevington. They relaunched the web site and now also run the Shetland News Agency, Shetland's only freelance news service. But that's not the end of it – in the belief that, if Orkney can have two weekly newspapers, so can Shetland, there are moves afoot to launch another Shetland weekly, *Shetland Today*. The project is backed by Malcolm Younger, a Shetland entrepreneur behind the monthly *Shetland Post* and the recently launched bi-monthly, *The Shetland Pictorial Post*.

Lewis and Harris

The Stornoway Gazette, which was founded in 1917, has a circulation of over 13,000 and has managed to see off the competition – in fact, it now owns what was the competition. In April 2003, two former editors of *The Stornoway Gazette* launched *The Hebridean* to compete with their old publication. It was a brave try but the publication lived for only nine months. Then *The Stornoway Gazette* bought the title and relaunched it. They are both published from the same office. *The Stornaway Gazette*, a broadsheet, comes out on the Thursday and *The Hebridean*, a tabloid with a circulation of 3,000, comes out on a Friday. As one reporter put it, 'We are in the same building and we are not supposed to be competitors but sometimes there are not many stories around.'

Skye

The West Highland Free Press is published in Broadford and is good at tackling national issues as they affect the islands. It has a circulation of around 9,547. It was founded in 1972 as a left-wing weekly newspaper and it certainly enjoys rattling cages.

Arran

The Arran Banner (which also happens to be the name of a well-known seed potato) is based in Brodick and was founded in 1974. It has a circulation of 3,750 and what it calls 'an exceptionally strong subscriber base'. In 2003, it was bought by *The Oban Times*.

Bute

The Buteman, published in Rothesay, was established in 1854 and has a circulation of around 3,500. It describes itself as essential reading for Brandanes, the name given to people born in Rothesay. Over the years, it has seen rivals come and go – *The Rothesay Chronicle* and *The Rothesay Express* did not last the pace.

Islay

The Ileach (pronounced 'eye lee') is the word for people born and bred on Islay. This has a strong following on Islay and has been published fortnightly for thirty-one years. Until 2003, it was published by the Islay Council of Social Services but it is now run independently by volunteers. They have introduced a new concept to the newspaper world – they have three editors who work in rotation. They print 2,500 copies each fortnight and the publication is available on-line. It claims to have the highest saturation coverage of any community newspaper and no one is going to argue with three editors.

Mull

Am Muileach (pronounced 'am moo lach' and meaning 'about Mull') is published monthly and you can credit – or blame – television for its birth. It has a most unusual mission statement. It was published in its first edition in November 1981 and tells you so much about island life. Here's an extract:

> A century ago, there would be a ceilidh house in each small village community on the island – a place where people naturally met to talk, exchange news, tell stories and sing songs. Today, there are no such places; each house has its own source of easy entertainment contained in a box which can be switched off. Ceilidhs are organised things, usually to raise money, with an audience singing in serried ranks. There seems to be nowhere now where everyone and anyone in the community, young or old, can meet to discuss common difficulties and interests or just to have a crack. It is hoped that this paper might come to be used as a modern equivalent of the old ceilidh house – where problems can be shared, ideas aired and where you're likely to find a good story or two.

Superb stuff and all these years later it is still taking the place of the old ceilidh house with a circulation of 1,200 and an estimated 2,800 loyal readers – copies being passed around, no doubt, when there is nothing decent on the telly. The publication is independently run by unpaid volunteers and it seems that one or two approaches have been made by 'incomers' to take it over – but they didn't know anything about the old ceilidhs and were shown the door.

Barra

Guhth Bharraidh (pronounced 'goo var eye' and meaning 'The Voice of Barra') is published by Voluntary Action Barra and Vatersay, a Council of Social Services organisation. It is a weekly publication with a circulation of between 650 and 750, which pretty well covers the island, but it also has readers in the UK and abroad. It has been going for more than twenty years.

Postage Stamps

Several Scottish islands issue or have issued their own postage stamps – they are called local stamps or are usually termed British Private Local Issues or Local Carriage Labels.

No official post offices operate on these islands and the stamps are issued ostensibly to cover the cost of ferrying mail to the nearest mainland post office. As these stamps are not officially recognised, they are not valid for international or national mail. Some philatelists do not recognise them either and regard them as no more than gimmicks but, nonetheless, they are island stamps and the islands that issue them or have issued them are listed in the Stanley Gibbons *British Commonwealth Stamp Catalogue*.

The islands that issue or have issued stamps are:

- Bernera from 1977
- Calve (off Mull) from 1984
- Canna (one of the Small Isles, west of Rum) from 1958
- Carn Iar (off the north-west coast) between 1961 and 1962
- Davaar (at the entrance of Campbeltown Loch) from 1964
- Easdale, Argyllshire, from 1988
- Eynhallow, Orkney, from 1973
- Gairsay, Orkney, from 1980
- Grunay, Shetland, from 1981
- Hestan, Wigtownshire, from the 1960s
- Hildasay, Shetland, from 1997
- Pabay, Skye, between 1962 and 1970, between 1972 and 1981 and from 1982
- St Kilda between 1968 and 1971
- Sanda, Argyllshire, between 1949 and 1970 and from 2004
- Shuna, Argyllshire, from 1949
- Soay, Skye, between 1965 and 1967
- Staffa, Hebrides, from 1969

- Stroma, Caithness, between 1962 and 1970 and from 1988
- Summer Isles, Hebrides, between 1970 and 1988 and from 1992

The 1970 Pabay stamps featured the Apollo moon landing in 1969. They are now collectors' items and are traded on the internet. The owners of Pabay, the Gannon family, have won a legal battle with the Royal Mail to be given permission to resume the issuing of island stamps.

The stamps issued by Soay, on St Kilda, have been declared bogus by the Committee of the Philatelic Traders Society.

Two islands have appeared on official Royal Mail stamps. Haroldswick on north-east Unst, in Shetland, featured in 1997 on a twenty-pence stamp in an issue released to mark the centenary of the National Federation of Sub-Postmasters. This was because it was Britain's most northerly post office and the Post Office Helpline, which gives you information about branches in the UK, still thinks it is. But, in fact, Haroldswick Post Office closed down just before the arrival of this century. Baltasound Post Office, also on Unst, is now Britain's most northerly post office. Sub-postmistress Valeria Johnson, who has had the Baltasound Post Office for six years, says she gets visits from philatelists from all over the world who want to have their letters and postcards franked with the words 'Baltasound – Britain's most northerly post office' plus a logo of two puffins. These eager philatelists have a long way to go – Lerwick itself, the Shetland capital, is far enough north but once they have got themselves there, they have to travel another sixty miles, with two ferry crossings, to get to Baltasound.

The Shetlands can lay claim to having some of the rarest stamps in the country.

Handwritten postmarks from some of the first letters posted in the Shetlands in 1842 have fetched thousands of pounds at auction. Letters were so rare in Shetland in 1842 that the Post Office had not yet issued a hand-stamp for there. So the local postmaster handwrote the places of origin – Brae, Tangwick and Voe – across the stamps on three envelopes as a way of cancellation. With no date stamp, experts dated the postmarks by matching the issue date of the stamps and handwriting of the postmaster with their 1840s records. These signatures across the stamps were enough to make a collector pay £4,140 for the three envelopes.

The other island to appear on a Royal Mail stamp is St Kilda. The island featured on a twenty-five-pence stamp that appeared in 1981 as part of an issue to mark the fiftieth anniversary of the National Trust for Scotland.

St Kilda can lay claim to having had the world's most unusual postal service. During the latter part of the eighteenth century, the main means of communication for the islanders was by way of little wooden vessels – known as the St Kilda mail boats – which contained a letter, usually sealed in a tin with a sheep's bladder acting as a float. They relied on the good nature of the trawlermen to pick up the inflated bladder and its message and make the delivery. The trawlermen seldom let them down and this unusual St Kilda mail boat saved the islanders from starvation on more than one occasion.

But, if you think that was unusual, this beats it. In 1934, a German rocket scientist, Gerhardt Zucher, somehow managed to persuade the British government that rockets could be used to transport mail and emergency medicines to remote islands. Amid much publicity, 30,000 letters were set to be launched into the Hebridean air from the small island of Scarp, off Harris. But the letter-laden rocket exploded before it got off the ground and that was its last post. Scarp, incidentally, did get a post office and at one time had a population of around 200. But depopulation set in – Scarp's only school closed in 1967, the post office shut down two years later and the last two families left the island in December 1971.

Transport

The Flannan Islands Lighthouse

Ferries and Planes

Ferries

Ferries are the lifeline of the Scottish islands, bringing in not only money-spending tourists but also the goods and provisions which keep the islanders going.

Caledonian MacBrayne

Known as CalMac, this company is the main provider of ferry services to the west-coast Scottish islands and has been for years. When the weather is unfavourable – yes, it does happen in Scotland – and the CalMac ferry is delayed or even cancelled, it has a knock-on effect which is felt throughout the islands involved. The sight of the CalMac ferry on its way into an island port is a welcome reassurance that all is well.

CalMac serves twenty-two Scottish islands and they are: Arran, Barra, Benbecula, Bute, Coll, Colonsay, Cowal, Cumbrae, Gigha, Eigg, Harris, Iona, Islay, Lewis, Lismore, Muck, Mull, North Uist, South Uist, Raasay, Skye and Tiree. Many of its fleet vessels are named after islands – *Eigg*, *Hebridean Isles*, *Isle of Arran*, *Isle of Cumbrae*, *Isle of Lewis*, *Isle of Mull* and *Raasay*.

The company was established in February 1851 and takes its name from those of its founders, David Hutcheson, Alexander Hutcheson and David MacBrayne, but it started life as David Hutcheson & Co. But it will perhaps come as a surprise to learn that CalMac was actually born as a result of tragedies that hit a man whose name has no association with the firm. That man was George Burns and he sold eight steamers, two trackboats and a fair amount of goodwill to what became CalMac.

According to *Royal Road to the Isles*, the official history of CalMac, George Burns sold those vessels because the burden of running his business had become too great in both personal and financial terms.

On 18 June 1850, one of his Liverpool ships, *The Orion*, had sunk off Portpatrick with great loss of life, including those of his brother and niece. His sister Elizabeth (Beth), who had married one David MacBrayne, died soon afterwards. Then, on 5 February 1851, the boiler of one of his ships, *The Plover*, burst while she was getting up steam in Glasgow. The engineer was killed and Burns decided it was time to get out and just five days later the sale was completed.

David Hutcheson was the company's chief clerk and had been running the Highland steamers for some time. Burns made one of the conditions of the sale that David MacBrayne, the late Beth's son, would be one of the partners. Thus the CalMac founding triumvirate, David Hutcheson, Alexander Hutcheson and David MacBrayne was created.

It was expansion and change thereafter, with heavy investment in vessels and the opening of new routes to cover the islands. The structure of the company has changed on a number of occasions but the objective – to serve Scotland's islands – has not.

Northlink Ferries

The company supplies the services to what some call the Northern Islands – Orkney and Shetland – with day sailings from Scrabster near Thurso to Stromness in Orkney, and nightly sailings from Aberdeen to Lerwick in Shetland. It used to be P&O Scottish Ferries which operated from the mainland to Orkney and Shetland but, in December 2000, the Scottish Executive appointed Northlink to take over the service. This took CalMac into northern waters – Northlink is a fifty–fifty joint venture between CalMac and the Royal Bank of Scotland. Northlink has not ruled out introducing a service to Orkney and Shetland from Rosyth in Fife.

When Northlink was established, it asked readers of the *Shetland Times* and *The Orcadian* and listeners of BBC Radio Shetland and BBC Radio Orkney to come up with names for the Northlink vessels. The winning names tell you much about the roots and loyalties of the islanders: *Hjatland* (the Old Norse name for Shetland), *Hrossey* (the Old Norse name for Orkney), *Hamnavoe* (Norse for 'home port' or 'save haven' and the old name for Stromness) and *Hascosay* (the name of an island off mainland Shetland).

Pentland Ferries

This ferry firm runs an attractive, alternative route to Orkney – a short crossing-time of one hour between Gills Bay, which is a brief drive from John O'Groats, and St Margaret's Hope on South Ronaldsay.

John O'Groats Ferries

Another route to Orkney is provided by John O'Groats Ferries. The sailing, which takes just forty minutes, leaves from John O'Groats and arrives at Burwick, on the southern tip of South Ronaldsay, where a bus is laid on to take passengers the twenty miles to Kirkwall. This ferry service is for passengers only (it can carry 250 passengers) and its emphasis is on day tours.

Once you get to the Northern Isles the local authorities take over with ferry services.

Orkney Ferries

This service is managed by Orkney Islands Council and runs ferries to Eday, Flotta, Graemsay, Hoy, North Ronaldsay, Egilsay, Rousay, Wyre, Sanday, Shapinsay, Stromsay, Westray and Papa Westray. You can even get an underwater view of sunken German battleships at Scapa Flow.

Shetland Ferries

Shetland Islands Council owns and operates a fleet of fourteen ferries from sixteen terminals to nine islands that have a total population of just under 3,500 people. The ships make over 70,000 crossings each year, carrying almost 700,000 passengers and over 300,000 vehicles. The islands served by Shetland Ferries are Yell, Unst, Fetlar, Whalsay, Bressay, Skerries, Fair Isle, Foula and Papa Stour.

Planes

The islands are well served by airlines, with airports at Barra, Benbecula, Islay, Kirkwall, Stornoway, Sumburgh in Shetland and Tiree.

Shetland Airstrips

FAIR ISLE
Magnificent scenery and matching knitwear

FETLAR
Known as the Garden of Shetland

FOULA
Thousands of seabirds and some of Britain's highest cliffs

OUT SKERRIES
Rare birds and fishing community

PAPA STOUR
Peace and wild flowers – supposedly once attracted a hippy colony

SCATSTA
Airport for Sullom Voe oil terminal

TINGWALL
Agricultural museum

UNST
Shetland's most northerly isle

WHALSAY
A recreation haven – fishing and golf on a nine-hole course

Orkney Airstrips

EDAY
Bird watcher's' paradise

FLOTTA
North Sea oil terminal – not a tourist haunt

NORTH RONALDSAY
Orkney's most northerly island where the ovine menu is unusual – *see* Unusual Eating Habits chapter

PAPA WESTRAY
Home to Arctic terns and skuas

SANDAY
Some of the finest beaches in Orkney

STRONSAY
Low-lying island with sandy beaches

WESTRAY
Strong fishing community

Lighthouses

The Northern Lighthouse Board covers half the waters and coastline of the United Kingdom, together with the majority of offshore manned oil installations. The area of responsibility is Scotland and the Isle of Man and that takes up 6,214 miles and a land area of 30,405 square miles – and no fewer than 790 islands.

There are over 200 lighthouses. Automation started in 1960 because of the high costs of manning lighthouses and, in 1998, Fair Isle South became the Northern Lighthouse Board's last manned lighthouse. Many of the lighthouses have a fascinating history and stories to tell and there are some wonderful names. And you do not have to delve very far into the history of Scottish lighthouses before you find the name Stevenson.

Robert Stevenson, born in Glasgow, in 1797 succeeded his stepfather as engineer to the Lighthouse Board. He held the post for forty-seven years and was responsible for designing eighteen of Scotland's lighthouses. Robert Stevenson, grandfather of the author Robert Louis Stevenson, began a dynasty of what was known as the Lighthouse Stevensons. Between 1790 and 1940, eight members of the family planned, designed and built ninety-seven lighthouses around the Scottish coast.

There is wonderment about the life, loneliness and danger of a lighthouse keeper and, although the lighthouses are now automated, the stories of the men and women who dedicated themselves to a lonely, harsh and sometimes dangerous way of life live on – and the lighthouses continue to save lives.

Island lighthouses (extracts from www.nlb.org.uk with permission of the Northern Lighthouse Board) are as follows:

Flannan Islands

In 1900, a year after it was established, this lighthouse took its place in the annals of mystery. In the stormy month of December, it became known that, for ten days, no light had been seen on the islands from the nearest point in Lewis, sixteen miles away. When the ship *Hesperus* arrived to change the shifts there was no sign of the three keepers, James Ducat, married with four children, Donald MacArthur, married with two children, and Thomas Marshall. The station was deserted, the lamp was trimmed and ready, the lens and machinery had been cleaned, the kitchen had been tidied and two sets of outdoor clothing were missing. No trace of the men was ever found. This, and the death a few years later of an assistant keeper injured by a fall when on duty, gave the Flannans an evil reputation.

Butt of Lewis

Built in 1862, the station became the radio link for the keepers on the isolated Flannan Isles in the early 1930s and continued to function as such until 1971 when the Flannans lighthouse was de-manned and the light became automated. Today, the Butt of Lewis acts as the monitoring station for the automatic light on the Flannans, North Rona and Sula Sgeir and is the radio control station for the North Minch area. The Butt of Lewis used to be manned by three keepers who lived at the station with their families. It was machine-gunned by a German aircraft in 1940. The station's claim to fame, according to the *Guinness Book of Records* some years ago, was that it was the windiest spot in the UK. It went automatic in 1995.

Tiumpan Head, Lewis

It opened at the start of the twentieth century. The Queen, Prince Charles and Princess Anne visited the lighthouse in 1956 when the seven-year-old heir to the throne sounded the first blast on a new fog siren. There were six keepers attached to the station with their families and two occasional keepers from the village nearby helped out. The lighthouse was automated in 1985.

Hyskeir

Situated five miles south-west of Canna and five miles west of Rum, this was established in 1904 to light the southern end of the Minch and to warn shipping off Mills Rocks, Canna Island and the rock on which the lighthouse was built. The families of the keepers lived in Oban and the keepers were taken out there by helicopter for their month of duty. The Moderator of the General Assembly of the Church of Scotland visited Hyskeir by helicopter in 1974. Although the keepers were taken to and from the rock by helicopter for their reliefs, heavy items such as oil and equipment had to be landed by the lighthouse vessel *Pharos*. During the winter of 1980, bad weather prevented the lighthouse vessel *Fingal* from delivering ten barrels of oil on a number of occasions between September and January. When the supplies were finally landed, only two days' supply of oil remained at the station. It went automatic in March 1997.

Copinsay, Orkney

The Copinsay light first came on in 1915. In recent years, the island has become a bird sanctuary but, in the 1930s, it was farmed by a Mr Groat who was a busy man. He was the father of thirteen children and he and the other keepers had so many children that there had to be a resident teacher on the island. One of the rooms in the farmhouse was the classroom. There is a group of three islands off the west coast of Copinsay which are accessible at low water – Ward Holm, Corn Holm and Black Holm. The bow of the trawler *Prince Deluge*, which ran aground and sank on Black Holm a number of years ago, has been washed back up and is now lying high and dry on Corn Holm. During the Second World War, a British aircraft crash-landed on Copinsay just below the lighthouse but it was dismantled and taken away. The light was automated in 1991.

Rona, near Raasay

In 1853, Lighthouse Commissioners' Engineer, David Stevenson, who had succeeded his brother Alan, prepared a list of the forty-five possible sites he believed would be desirable to complete a system of lights for the coasts of Scotland – and Rona was one of them. It was one of five lighthouses whose lights first shone in November 1857 – and it was quite a change from what had previously alerted mariners. On Rona, a widow named Janet Mackenzie had, for many years, shown a light in one of her windows, enabling fishing boats to clear rocks at the harbour entrance. She was given a grant of £20 by the Commissioners.

Ornsay, off Skye

Its light first shone in 1857 and it was automated in 1962. In 1966 Gavin Maxwell Enterprises – of *Ring of Bright Water* fame – bought the cottages at Ornsay and at Kyleakin. Maxwell was drawn to them as he enjoyed planning and converting houses and he thought they had commercial possibilities. He converted them into holiday accommodation. The Ornsay cottage has four bedrooms and a 27-ft sitting-room which looks out on the Sound of Sleat and, of course, is next to a light which has a superb range of ten miles.

Eilean Glas, off Scalpay

This light first came on in 1789 and it was one of the first four lighthouses built in Scotland. When Alexander Reid, the first keeper at Eilean Glas, was pensioned off with an annuity of forty guineas in 1823, the engineer reported him to be 'weather-beaten and stiff by long exposure on the Point of Glas'. The lighthouse became automatic in 1978.

Barra Head, off Mingulay

Switched on in 1833, Barra Head, on the edge of a steep cliff on the island of Berneray, became automatic in 1980. After the

Second World War, the remains of a Blenheim bomber were found on the cliff face. The parts found enabled the Blenheim and crew to be identified – but no one had heard the crash.

Rinns of Islay, on the island of Orsay, off Islay

Established in 1825 and changed in 1978 to a sealed beam light mounted on a gearless revolving pedestal – a real step forward in lighthouse illumination – the station was automated in 1998.

Ruvaal, off Islay

This lighthouse was switched on in 1859. In February 1981, the lighthouse helicopter was helping to connect a main power line from Islay to Ruvaal. The first two poles had been successfully landed but, when the helicopter tried to land the third, the pole struck the main rotor and destroyed it. The helicopter crashed, ending up with the broken stump of the pole lying across the tail boom. The pilot had a remarkable escape.

Dubh Artach, on the island of Erraid

The need for a lighthouse here was underlined between December 1865 and January 1866 when storms of unprecedented ferocity wrecked or drove ashore twenty-four vessels in the areas bounded by Tiree, Iona, Colonsay and Islay. There were petitions for the erection of a lighthouse and, after the Commissioners had examined the records of wrecks, they agreed – but it was easier said than done. Although Board of Trade sanction was given in 1866, it was 1872 before the lighthouse was completed. Bad weather plagued the building work – in 1870, there were sixty-two landings between April and October, but bad weather restricted the real working season to June, July and August. Nine houses were built for the families of the keepers and the crew of the attending steamer.

Skerryvore, about ten miles south-west of Tiree

The purpose of this lighthouse was alerting mariners to what is described as 'a very extensive and treacherous reef of rocks'. Building it was a mammoth task and it took six years from 1838. It was built of granite quarried from Mull and is regarded as an outstanding example of lighthouse engineering. Two to three dozen men were employed on the rock, often working seventeen-hour days, and more than double that number were employed on Mull to quarry the granite. The massive blocks of stone were shipped to Tiree where a further workforce dressed and shaped the stones so that, when they were landed on the rock, each would fit perfectly on to and into adjoining sets. The first Skerrymore light beamed out on 1 February 1884 and, in 1994, Skerrymore was automated.

Sanda, off Kintyre

After years of clamour for a lighthouse on this island, one was finally built in 1850. In 1900, the RNO silver medal and vellum citation was presented to the attending staff of Sanda – Daniel Dempsey and his two sons – for saving the crew of a schooner wrecked near the lighthouse, using a small boat in heavy seas and at great risk to themselves. One of the Northern Lighthouse Board's ships, the *Signal*, ran aground in dense fog in 1895 while on her way to Sanda. All on board, including one of the Commissioners, Sheriff William Ivory, were saved with most of their effects. Attempts to salvage the ship proved fruitless and she sank the next day. There have been several shipwrecks at Sanda. In March 1946, an American liberty ship ran aground with fifty-four people on board and all were saved. In October 1970, a Dutch cattle ship went aground. The cargo of livestock were either drowned or destroyed by SSPCA officers who flew out to Sanda by helicopter.

Ailsa Craig, Firth of Clyde

This lighthouse was established in 1886. Until wireless communications were established on Ailsa Craig in 1935, the keepers and employees of Ailsa Granites Ltd used to depend on pigeons for conveying their messages. The pigeons were provided by the lighthouse boatman, who received an annual payment of £4 for his trouble. When a doctor or supplies were required urgently in stormy weather, when it would be impossible to use the carrier pigeon, a system of signals by fire were used. One fire on the castle path showing the lighthouse to the north meant 'bring doctor to the lighthouse'; two fires on the path twenty–thirty yards apart meant 'bring doctor to the quarry company'; one fire showing the lighthouse to the south indicated that provisions were required. And the quarry company? For years Ailsa Craig rock has been used for curling stones – and, in particular, for the stones used by the women's team when they won the Winter Olympics 2002 Gold.

Pladda, off Arran

Pladda was first lit in 1790 and, in 1876, it became the third station to have a fog signal. Provisions and other light stores were brought to the lighthouse by boatmen permanently attached to the station and they also carried out reliefs. All this changed in 1972 with the introduction of helicopters. The station became automatic in 1990 and the keepers were withdrawn.

North Ronaldsay

This was the third lighthouse to be built in Scotland, first flashing its light in 1789, but, by 1806, it was considered redundant and switched off. However, after a few years it became obvious that the island, with its dangerous shoals, still required its own lighthouse so in 1852 it was decided to build another one. The current one is still the highest land-based lighthouse in the British Isles, soaring to a height of 139 feet. It was automated in 1998.

Pentland Skerries

This lighthouse, established in 1794, is listed as a building of architectural and historical interest. It was built when the Pentland Firth was opened to shipping in place of the longer route round Orkney. When the wife and seven children of the Principal Lightkeeper went down with diphtheria in 1877, two of the children died and were laid in what has been called 'one of the loneliest, saddest graveyards in the world', amid the swirling tides of the Pentland Firth. In 1871, a Royal Humane Society bronze medal for saving life at sea went to assistant Donald Montgomery off Pentland Skerries for rescuing a boy in what was described as the 'boiling tideway' off the east side of the island after the crew of the ship *Good Design* had taken to their lifeboat and the boy got into difficulty. When the *Vicksburg* went aground in the Pentland Skerries in 1884 and nine men died, four keepers saved twelve lives at much personal risk and danger. When the Principal Lightkeeper was taken ill during stormy weather in 1929, two young assistants never let the light or fog horn fail for the twelve days it took before a landing was possible. It was in the Pentland Skerries that the eight-man crew of the Longhope lifeboat, called out to help a drifting Liberian steamer, lost their lives in 1969. The steamer's crew of seventeen were rescued but the result was seven widows and ten orphans on Orkney.

Stroma, off Caithness

There are particularly turbulent seas around here because of the meeting of four or five contrary tides, known as the Merry Men of Mey. Off Stroma there is The Swilkie, the most dangerous whirlpool in the Pentland Firth. According to Icelandic legend, The Swilkie is the place where the salt which maintains the saltiness of the oceans is ground in a giant quern, which was stolen from King Frodi by a sea king named Mysing. When Mysing's longship sank off Stroma under the weight of it, he still continued to grind away with it at fifteen fathoms down and, to this day, the sea can still be heard roaring through it. In 1941 the lighthouse buildings were machine-gunned by an enemy plane. No one was injured and the keepers were able to repair the little damage done.

Cantick Head, Hoy

Established in 1858 and automated in 1991, it is now remotely controlled from the Northern Lighthouse Board's offices in Edinburgh. The lighthouse, the keepers' cottages, sundial pedestal and outbuildings are listed Grade B in terms of architectural and historic interest.

Sule Skerry

About forty miles west of Orkney, this one lies in the track of vessels passing through the Pentland Firth to or from the Iceland seas. It has the distinction of being listed by the *Guinness Book of Records* as having been the remotest manned lighthouse in Britain – until it became fully automatic in December 1982. It was built between 1892 and 1894 by David A. Stevenson and his brother Charles. During its construction, winter work was ruled out because of the short amount of daylight and the danger posed by stormy weather; but an exceptionally fine summer in 1893 allowed time lost to be made up. On many occasions it was cut off for days because of heavy seas. From 1973 the lighthouse keepers were relieved fortnightly by helicopters.

Muckle Flugga, off Unst, Shetland

The establishment of a lighthouse at Muckle Flugga, the most northerly rock in the British Isles, was considered by the Commissioners as far back as 1851 but, because of difficulties in determining where the exact site of the lighthouse should be, by 1854, no work had started on it. During the Crimean War, the Commissioners were urged by the government to erect a light at Muckle Flugga with a view to protecting Her Majesty's ships. A temporary lighthouse building taking just twenty-six days to erect was then completed and, by 1858, there was a permanent light. It was a particularly busy lighthouse during the Second World War. There were three keepers working at the one time. They spent one month on and one month off but heavy seas sometimes made departure long overdue. Robert Louis Stevenson visited Muckle Flugga in 1869 with his father, Thomas Stevenson, engineer to the Board, and there is a school of thought that the island of Unst influenced him in his writing of *Treasure Island*.

Esha Ness, on Shetland

Established in 1929, this was the last Northern Lighthouse Board manned facility to be designed by a member of the Stevenson family – David A. Stevenson, the engineer for the station. The station was automated in 1974 and sold to a private owner.

Out Skerries, off Shetland

The first light was a temporary structure built on the island of Grunay in 1854 at the request of the Royal Navy when it was engaged in the Crimean War. During the Second World War the lighthouse was machine-gunned in 1941 but the Germans came back with a vengeance a year later. A single enemy bomber approached the island from the west at a low level and passed directly over the lighthouse dwellings. One or two bombs were dropped, missed the buildings and fell into the sea. The raider made a wide circle, returned over the buildings and dropped another bomb which made a direct hit on the boatman's house. The house was completely demolished and the only occupant at the time, the boatman's mother, was buried beneath the debris, sustaining injuries from which she died in Lerwick on 20 January 1942.

Bressay, off Shetland

Situated on the island of Bressay, this lighthouse was opened in 1858 and became automated in 1989. In 1995, the out-buildings and former keepers' cottages were bought by the Shetland Amenity Trust, a charitable organisation set up to conserve and enhance Shetland's heritage. Two cottages have been refurbished and are available on a short-term lease, one cottage is now a self-catering holiday home and the engine and radio rooms are being turned into a heritage centre.

Sumburgh Head, on Shetland

There's a sleepy tale about this one. The most serious offence a keeper can commit is falling asleep on watch, as this might allow a light to be unexpectedly extinguished, be less efficient or inadvertently change – in other words, you've got to keep an eye on the light at all times, just in case. There were fifteen cases of keepers falling asleep at the wrong time in the second half of the nineteenth century but the worst was here at Sumburgh in 1871 when it was discovered by later confession that two keepers agreed not to report each other for sleeping at their posts. One of them was the Principal Keeper with twenty-three years' service – and both were dismissed.

Foula, off Shetland

Established in 1986, this was never a manned station and it was built as a direct result of the increase in oil-tanker traffic using the west-coast route.

Fair Isle South, off Shetland

This lighthouse was established in 1892. During an air attack in December 1941, the wife of the assistant keeper, Mrs Sutherland, was killed and her infant daughter was slightly hurt. Six weeks after this, the wife and daughter of the principal keeper were killed when a second air attack produced a direct hit on the main dwelling block – and the raid also put the light out. Roderick Macaulay, assistant keeper at Fair Isle North (where he and his daughter had had a narrow escape in a previous attack), walked three miles through snowdrifts and gale-force winds to help restore the vital light and he then walked back in the dark to take his own regular watch. He received the BEM for his outstanding services. A plaque in memory of the war dead was erected by the Northern Lighthouse Board and Scotland's Lighthouse Museum on the boundary wall of the station in 1998. This was Scotland's last manned lighthouse, having become automated on 31 March 1998.

Fair Isle North

This one was also a target during the Second World War. In March 1941, the lighthouse houses were machine-gunned by an enemy plane. Two bombs were dropped with little damage but, less than a month later, the enemy was back and dropped two bombs which were direct hits, causing considerable damage.

Bass Rock, off East Lothian

Established in 1903, it lies close to the ruins of a pre-Reformation chapel which was dedicated to St Baldred and was consecrated in the year 1542. The Bass Rock has a long and varied history. It is mentioned in writings dating back to the reign of Malcolm Canmore and the first recorded owner of the island was Sir Robert Lauder, who was granted a charter for it around 1316. At one time, the island was a prison for Presbyterian ministers and, between 1672 and 1688, some forty political or religious prisoners died in the rock dungeons. In 1691, a party of four Jacobite prisoners escaped from their cells and captured the fortress. For the next three years, they held the Bass for the Old Pretender and defied all attempts by government forces to retake it. Aided by supply ships from France, this quartet even carried out raids on Fife and Lothian. In 1694, an effective blockage finally starved them into submission, but they negotiated favourable terms and walked away free men. Until the First World War, the rock was let out to tenants who earned money by fishing, grazing sheep – Bass mutton was a famous eighteenth-century delicacy – and by killing young seabirds and collecting eggs. The lighthouse was automated in 1988 and the true owners of the rock are the birds, with almost every available inch occupied by razorbills, guillemots, cormorants, puffins, eider ducks and various gull species. It also has a colony of 30,000–40,000 pairs of gannet. The rock is now a Mecca for international ornithologists.

Visitors to the Seabird Centre in North Berwick can view the birds on the Bass Rock via a live camera link that allows them to manipulate the cameras themselves and so follow the activities of any bird that is of particular interest to them.

Inchkeith

The island of Inchkeith lies roughly between Leith and King-horn. It has, in its time, been the seat of Pictish kings, a base for early Christian evangelists, an isolation colony for those stricken by the plague, a medieval fortress, a victim of siege and blockade, the scene of a gory battle, a site for heavy guns during two world wars – and home to a lighthouse opened in 1804.

Bell Rock

This is the oldest existing rock lighthouse in the British Isles – the Bell Rock is a long and treacherous reef lying in the North Sea some twelve miles east of Dundee. It has always been a danger to navigation. In his account of the Bell Rock Lighthouse, Robert Stevenson, engineer to the Board, stated:

> There is a tradition that an Abbot of Aberbrothock directed a bell to be erected on the Rock, so connected with a floating apparatus that the winds and sea acted upon it and tolled the bell, thus giving warning to the mariner of his approaching danger. Upon similar authority the bell, it is said, was afterwards carried off by pirates and the humane intentions of the Abbot thus frustrated.

The erection of a permanent seamark on the Bell Rock pre-sented some difficult structural problems but it was estab-lished in 1811 and was the first revolving light in Scotland. On 27 October 1915, the captain of the *Argyll*, one of the Devonshire class of cruisers, sent a routine signal to the admi-ral commanding the coast of Scotland at Rosyth, requesting the Bell Rock to be lit on the night of 27/28 October. The message was never passed on as the lighthouse had no radio and all messages had to be delivered by boat. But heavy seas made this impossible and it was these heavy seas that sank the *Argyll* although there were no casualties among the 655 men.

In the Second World War, the lighthouse was machine-gunned three times by enemy aircraft and it was also bombed. Tragedy struck the Bell Rock in 1955 when the crew of an RAF helicopter was lost when seeking to drop gifts to the keepers as a goodwill gesture. The friendly flashing light was extinguished as a result of the accident. This was probably the only time the light was not exhibited in its 158 years – apart from those times during the war years, when it was deliberately left unlit to make things difficult for the enemy. The lighthouse was demanned in 1988.

Fidra

The lighthouse is on the small rocky island of Fidra in the Firth of Forth off the East Lothian coast. As well as the lighthouse, there are the remains of a chapel. Fidra is noted for its large colony of puffins. The island is a designated RSPB Reserve. Described in Robert Louis Stevenson's novel *Catriona*, Fidra is part of a basalt sill that was injected between the surrounding rocks by volcanic activity some 335 million years ago.

Isle of May

There's not one but two lighthouses on this rugged island several miles offshore from Anstruther in Fife. The Commissioners bought the island in 1815 and started building the present lighthouse. Not far away from it are the remains of the original lighthouse. It was built in 1635 and, at the time, it was the first and only lighthouse in Scotland. It was no more than a platform, twelve metres high, with a burning beacon on it. Ships were charged for the light and this enabled an improvement to be made on the design of the lighthouse to take the platform to eighteen metres. The charges – four Scottish shillings for foreign ships and two shillings for home vessels – were collected by customs officers on the Fife coast and brought in about £280 sterling each year. The light came from burning a ton of coal each night and, when gales were blowing, up to three tons of coal were consumed. When there was a gale, little of the light could be seen on the dangerous westward side. In January 1791, the light was out for two nights during a severe storm and a tragedy lay behind the absence of the light. The keeper, his wife and five of their children had been asphyxiated by the fumes – although a baby did survive.

Shipwrecks

The data that is produced by the Royal Commission on the Ancient and Historical Monuments of Scotland (RCAHMS) has a heading entitled 'Maritime' and there you will find listed most of the shipwrecks off the coast of Scotland. You can take a surfing exploratory dive into it if you wish but, be warned, a lot of it is boring and technical and does not have much interest unless you are a mariner wanting to steer clear of danger.

But if you were to sift through the mass of information, as we have done for you, you will find the stories, the drama and the tragedies, and they are all fascinating reminders of the perils at sea. Much of the wreckage off the Scottish islands is the result of the First and Second World Wars and it was action by German submarines that caused the most damage. And the biggest collection of wrecks is in Scapa Flow in Orkney where, on 21 June 1919, on the order of Rear Admiral Ludwig von Reuter, the whole German fleet of seventy-four warships was scuttled.

So, courtesy of the RCAHMS, join us on this journey among some of the shipwrecks off the Scottish islands.

Greian Head, Barra

ADELAAR

The scattered remains of this Dutch East Indiaman, wrecked in 1728, were found in 1972 around the exposed reef known locally as *Maolach Sgeir* (The Cursed Reef). There were no structural remains but what was found included five types of gun, sixty lead ingots, shot, iron tools, nails, a copper pan, fishing hooks, belt buckles, part of a pocket watch, clay pipe fragments and four pieces of gold jewellery. They are to go to an appropriate museum after discussion with the Dutch government.

Barra

ANNIE JANE

This was an emigrant ship on a voyage from Liverpool to Canada in September 1853 with 450 passengers and crew when she was struck by a huge wave in rough weather off Barra. The vessel went to pieces within fifteen minutes and 348 lives were lost.

Stilamair, off the south coast of Scalpay

BOSTON HERO

A steel trawler out of Milford Haven, this vessel got into difficulties south of Stilamair in December 1962. The island is populated by sheep and is one of the many small islands around Scalpay. Despite the ferocious sea, six men from Scalpay immediately set out in an open boat to try to give assistance They managed to rescue four of the trawlermen, one of whom was clinging exhausted to the rocks, but they were unable to save the other seven. Their heroism was recognised by gallantry awards from the RNLI.

Baltasound, Unst

E39

The vessel's name is all letters and numbers but that's typical of the tragedies of the two World Wars. It belongs to a submarine which was mined with the loss of three officers and twenty-eight ratings. The mine is thought to have been laid during the First World War by the German submarine *UC76*. *E39* was built by Swan Hunter on the Tyne under the emergency war programme, between 1913 and 1916, and it is now a war grave.

Skerryvore, off Tiree

RAVENSHEUGH

This was a Glasgow steamer on a voyage to Riga with coal and
it got into difficulty in November 1911. The skipper, Captain
Daniels, the first and second mates, first and second engineers,
the donkeyman, an able seaman and a fireman all perished,
along with the cook and a steward. Daniels and nine of the
crew stuck with the ship until she went down. There were nine
survivors.

Coll and Tiree

NESSMORE

This one was a real find. The story has all the elements of
Whisky Galore. The vessel was on its way from Montreal to
Liverpool in November 1895 when it got into difficulty in the
sound between Coll and Tiree. There were 550 cattle on board
and part of the cargo of 4,000 tons were 20,000 cheeses. The
crew of fifty were all saved and the cattle were put ashore on
Coll. According to *The Oban Times* of 30 November 1895:

> On being thrown overboard, the majority of the cattle swam
> the half mile between the vessel and the shore. A few are
> said to have reached Tiree. Others were drowned. A difficulty
> arose as to whether the cattle, for which there was no
> certificate, could be landed on Coll where so many animals
> were kept for dairy purposes. The local sanitary inspector has
> wired the procurator fiscal for instructions. We understand
> that the Board of Agriculture have granted authority for the
> re-shipment of the cattle from the port of Coll.

The newspaper returned to the subject on 4 December 1895:

> A fortnight's storm and the Atlantic swell have now almost
> battered the NESSMORE to pieces. Were it not for the sake of
> saving a valuable steam engine and a pump worth about

£400 which was still on board the wreck, Captain Young of the Salvage Association would have left the scene some days ago. The Coll and Tiree people were not seemingly to get all the spoils, notwithstanding its proximity to their shores. The westerly winds which have prevailed generally during the week have driven large quantities of the wreckage – cheese, flour, apples and even American organs to the north-west coast of Mull, the shores of Gometra and the Treshnish Islands. Gometra has been favoured with a musical instrument, Quinish with cheese and a vast abundance of apples. The flour which has been washed ashore is said to be in a wonderfully preserved state, the salt water in many cases not having penetrated more than half an inch.

Duart Point, Mull

SWANN

This shipwreck was found close to the shore in 1979. She was a small ship, with various elements of timber structure, and the finds indicate a mid seventeenth-century date. These finds include part of a pistol lock, a pocket watch, a sword hilt, clay pipe and a leather shoe. Some of the finds, it is said, indicate the presence on board of high-status individuals and human remains have been found. Who were they? Nobody knows. Later detective work indicated that the vessel was the *Swann*, a small warship lost during Cromwell's suppression of the Earl of Glencairn's revolt in support of the Royalist cause in 1653. She was one of six Cromwellian warships sent to root out Royalist sympathisers and was apparently one of three from a flotilla of six which were sunk in a storm.

Rathin Island

TUSCANIA

This Anchor Line vessel, built in 1914, was torpedoed and sunk by a German submarine. The vessel had been taken over as war transport and was carrying 2,030 American troops from Halifax to Liverpool. In all, 166 lives were lost.

Islay

EXMOUTH

This vessel, full of emigrants, was on her way from Londonderry to Quebec on 28 April 1847 when she hit bad weather off Islay and went down. There were only three survivors out of a total of 254 passengers and crew.

Orkney

HMS HAMPSHIRE

This is a biggie in the history books – this armed cruiser was detached from the Grand Fleet for the special duty of conveying Lord Kitchener and his staff to Russia. She left Scapa Flow on 5 June 1916 and struck a mine off Brough Head, Birsay. Of the complement of 655 men and seven passengers, only 12 men survived. Lord Kitchener and his staff all perished and the wreck is now a designated war grave.

SVINTO

This one did not have much luck – she was abandoned after an attack by aircraft in March 1940 while en route from Preston to Oslo. She was taken in tow by a tug – but was torpedoed and sunk by a German submarine about five miles off Copinsay.

Auskerry, Orkney

SS HASTINGS COUNTY

Built in America in 1920, this vessel went aground in fog in
June 1926 while attempting to make the Fair Isle passage en
route from Hamburg to Montreal. The mixed cargo was large-
ly toys and teddy bears and two luxury motor pinnaces, carried
as deck cargo. Apart from a few teddies, all was subsequently
salvaged, along with most of its valuable bunker coal.

North Ronaldsay, Orkney

SVECIA

This is quite a yarn. The *Svecia* was an armed merchantman of
twenty-eight guns. Based at Gothenburg, she was carrying 600
tons of cargo belonging to the Swedish East India Company.
In 1739, on her second voyage, she went to Bengal to collect
merchandise from a small Swedish factory there and, in 1740,
she sailed for home. Contemporary accounts suggest that the
cargo was worth between £150,000 and £250,000, which, at
that time, was an enormous sum. On the way to Bengal – or,
perhaps, once they got there – the captain plus about forty of
the 140 people on board died. And, on the way back, the vessel, intending to pass between the Orkneys and the Fair Isle,
was caught in a storm and ended up trapped on a notorious
submerged rock between Sanday and North Ronaldsay.

But their troubles were not over. The ship stayed stuck on
that rock for three days while the passengers tried to save
themselves. The islanders of North Ronaldsay made no
attempt to approach the stricken ship, even though she was
only one-and-a-half miles off the south-east tip of the island.
They were denounced for this by the survivors as 'barbarous
savages' but it has to be said that the islanders' boats were too
small to take the risk in such a severe storm. The longboat and
yawl were launched and thirty-one of the passengers made it

to the Fair Isle. Those still on board the *Svecia* used topmasts and rigging to make a raft and thirty of them of them made off – and disappeared. That left twenty-four on the vessel and they put another raft together. The raft made it to North Ronaldsay but with only thirteen of them remaining. There were thus only forty-four survivors of the total of 104 who were believed to have been on board at the time of the wreck. A fierce gale which followed tore open hundreds of bales of Bengal cotton and silk and left the material on the shores of North Ronaldsay. As Hereditary Admiral of the Orkneys and Shetlands James, Earl of Morton, claimed a proportion of the salvage. So did the Swedish East India Company and they managed to recover over 200,000 yards of cloth between them despite the rival attentions of the islanders and incomers.

Isle of May, Forth Estuary

AVONDALE PARK

On her way from Hull to Belfast, this vessel was torpedoed and sunk by a German submarine. She was the last Allied ship to be sunk by a German submarine in the European theatre of war.

Mull

THE TOBERMORY GALLEON

This wreck one is not in the RCAHMS list but it has to be included. Its story begins with the English rout of the Spanish Armada in the English Channel in 1588. After the battle, the Spanish fleet was scattered and many of them chose to sail for home round the north of Scotland. One of the Spanish ships arrived in Tobermory in late September or October 1588 to renew her sails, which had been reduced to tatters as a result of the close attention of the English warships which were backed up by the Scottish weather. In November 1588, when anchored in Tobermory Bay, the vessel was hit by a mighty explosion which destroyed her and sent her to the bottom, leaving only fifty to sixty Spaniards alive.

From the day the ship went down, the legend of the Tobermory Treasure began. There have been dozens of attempts to salvage the wreck but there has been little success in finding anything of value.

Transport – of Sorts

Vatersay and Barra

It's thanks to Bernie that there is a causeway linking Vatersay and Barra. Farmers had campaigned for some time to get this causeway so that it would be easier for them to take their cattle to the market – certainly a lot easier than having to swim them across the Sound of Vatersay to meet the ferry and their fate. Then, in 1986, Bernie, a prize bull, drowned while swimming to the ferry and the resultant publicity made the government come up with the £3.8 million that was needed for the causeway. It was completed in 1990.

Rothesay

Rothesay is the only Scottish island to have had a tram service. It was electrified in 1902 but buses eventually took over in 1934.

Colonsay and Oronsay

These two islands are separated by a wide expanse of shell sand called The Strand. When the tide is out, you can walk or drive across it or you can hitch a lift on a Post Office bus. But make sure your timepiece is in good condition – the tide could trap you. This unusual delivery service by the Post Office has been under threat but it still survives and the chat with the driver is a bonus.

Seil

When you go over to Seil, it is a short but memorable journey – to get there, you cross what is proudly known as the only bridge over the Atlantic. It is called the Clachan Bridge and was designed by Thomas Telford. It has an unusual permanent guest in its old masonry – a rare and tiny foxglove which is native to central Europe. How it found its way to Seil and the Atlantic crossing no one knows. Close to the bridge and well worth a stop for a refreshment is the hotel known as the *Tigh na Truish*, the House of Trousers. During the time when wearing Highland dress was banned by law, after the Jacobite rebellion, shore-going islanders would swap their kilts in this hotel for a pair of trousers.

Raasay

Raasay has the road that Calum built. When the local authority refused to build a road to his town of Arnish, Calum MacLeod was not a happy man. He reckoned that this was the cause of his town's depopulation and he decided to do something about it. No, not by fathering more children, but by building the road himself. Armed with a small book on road building and a sackful of determination, he built 3,000 yards of tarred road that twisted and turned its way to Arnish. During this mammoth undertaking, he wore out two wheelbarrows, six picks, six shovels, four spades and five hammers but not his patience and endeavour – he kept right on to the end of the road and it took him ten years to build this single-track thoroughfare with passing places.

When he started that lonesome road, there were seven families in the area. When he finished, there was no one left except him and his wife. Calum, a postman and an acclaimed Gaelic scholar, died in 1988 when working on the final part of the road which was to finish at his front door. He was awarded the British Empire Medal for his efforts and the Calum MacLeod Memorial Cairn was erected at the side of the road he built in recognition of his single-mined determination.

Was it all worth it? Mrs Rebecca Mackay, secretary and treasurer of the Raasay Heritage Trust, told me:

It certainly was – there is now a family living at Arnish. Calum's road has opened up the north of the island and has led to a fish farm being established in that part of Raasay. That has meant jobs and other benefits for the island. Also, the road has become something of a tourist attraction.

Kirkwall

Kirkwall must be the only town to display a red triangular road sign that says, 'Otters crossing 100 yards'.

Barra

Barra has a unique airport – its runway disappears under the sea twice every day. The planes land and take off from the crunchy shell sands known as the Cockle Strand. The cockles and cockleshells are useful for harling and are gathered in for that purpose. In 1994, tractors were introduced to make the cockle extraction more efficient but it was soon reckoned that the effects of this were not good for landing planes, whose schedules had to be flexible because of the tide times. The tractors were banned and it was back to the traditional hand-raking.

Westray and Papa Westray

These Orkney islands are connected by the world's shortest scheduled flight – it lasts just two minutes, even less with a following wind.

Mull

On Mull, there is a miniature steam railway. It runs on a narrow gauge from Craignure's old pier along the shore and through the woods to the early Victorian Torosay Castle that David Bryce designed in 1858. The Mull Rail is the only working railway in the Scottish islands.

The Small Isles

Resident motorists of The Small Isles – Eigg, Muck, Canna and Rum – are granted a special privilege by the Vehicle and Operator Services Agency – their vehicles do not have to undergo a Ministry of Transport (MOT) test. The Small Isles are notorious for their old bangers that would certainly not pass the government test and many islanders keep two cars –

an island runabout and a more reliable one which will keep them on the right side of the law should they visit the mainland. Eigg has a population of eighty people with thirty MOT-free vehicles that use a road less than ten miles long.

Bibliography

Burke, John, *A Traveller's History of Scotland* (London: John Murray, 1990)

Crowl, Philip A., *An Intelligent Traveller's Guide to Historic Scotland* (London: Sidgwick & Jackson, 1986)

Devlin, Vivien, *Scottish Island Hopping* (Edinburgh: Polygon, 1999)

Fabian, Derek J., Graham E. Little and D. Noel Williams, *The Islands of Scotland including Skye* (The Scottish Mountaineering Trust, 1989)

Haswell-Smith, Hamish, *The Scottish Islands, A Comprehensive Guide to Every Scottish Island* (Canongate: Edinburgh, 2004)

Humphries, Rob and Donald Reid, *Scotland, The Rough Guide* (London: Rough Guides, 2002)

Jackson, Michael, *Michael Jackson's Malt Whisky Companion* (London: Dorling Kindersley, 2003)

Keay John and Julia Keay (eds), *Collins Encyclopaedia of Scotland* (London: HarperCollins, 1994)

Lindsay, Maurice, *The Castles of Scotland* (London: Constable, 1986)

McCrorie, Ian, *Royal Road to the Isles* (Gourock: Caledonian MacBrayne Ltd, 2001)

Miers, Richenda, *Scotland: Highlands & Islands* (London: Cadogan Guides, 1994)

Moss, Michael S. and John R. Hume, *The Making of Scotch Whisky* (Edinburgh: James and James, 1981)

Munro, R. W., *Scottish Lighthouses* (Stornoway: Thule Press, 1979)

Newton, Norman, *Roads to the Isles* (Moffat: House of Lochar Publishing, 1991)

Noonan, Damien, *Castles & Ancient Monuments of Scotland* (London: Aurum Press, 2000)

Owen, Olwyn, *The Sea Road* (Edinburgh: Canongate, 1999)

Pendreigh, Brian, *Pocket Scottish Movie Book* (Edinburgh: Mainstream Publishing, 2002)

Perrott, D., *Western Island Handbook* (Montgomeryshire: Kittiwake Press, 1998)

Ritchie, Anna, *Viking Scotland* (London: B. T. Batsford, 1993)

Ritchie, Anna, *Orkney and Shetland – Exploring Scotland's Heritage* (Edinburgh: Her Majesty's Stationery Office, 1985)

Robb, J. Marshall, *Scotch Whisky: A Guide* (Edinburgh: W. & R. Chambers, 1950)

Rodger, Stokes and Ogilvie, *Heritage Trees of Scotland* (Wetherby: Forestry Commission Publications, 2003)